EDITOR: MARTIN

OSPREY
MILITARY

ELITE SE

SOLDIERS OF THE ENGLISH CIVIL WAR 2 CAVALRY

Text by
JOHN TINCEY
Colour plates by
ANGUS McBRIDE

First published in Great Britain in 1990 by
Osprey, an imprint of Reed Consumer Books Ltd.
Michelin House, 81 Fulham Road,
London SW3 6RB
and Auckland, Melbourne, Singapore and Toronto

British Library Cataloguing in Publication Data
Tincey, John
    Soldiers of the English Civil war. – (Elite series)
    1. English civil war. Military forces
    I. Title · II. McBride, Angus   III. Series 942.06′2

    ISBN 0-85045-940-0.

Filmset in Great Britain
Printed through World Print Ltd, Hong Kong

If you would like to receive more information about
Osprey Military books, The Osprey Messenger is a
regular newsletter which contains articles, new title
information and special offers. To join free of charge
please write to:

**Osprey Military Messenger,
PO Box 5, Rushden,
Northants NN10 6YX**

Author's Note

This book examines how the soldiers of 1642 expected
to fight the Civil Wars; and how experience changed
their ideas. The work of theorists who wrote before,
during and after the war has been studied, along with
the experiences of those who fought in the wars.
Unfortunately, few 17th century soldiers wrote
memoirs, and those who did sought only to defend or
advertise their own actions. Despite new research,
many books still reproduce Victorian illustrations of
'Cavaliers and Roundheads' without question. The
colour plates that appear in this book challenge many
preconceived ideas. Their technical and artistic merit is
due to Angus McBride, but I take responsibility for
their conception and any mistakes therein.

I would like to thank all the contributors to the
magazine *English Civil War Notes & Queries* who
provided invaluable information which helped to
shape this book. I must also acknowledge my debt to
Gail, who has transformed the text into readable
English.

Artist's Note

Soldiers of the English Civil War (2): Cavalry

Cavalry

The Theorists

At the start of the Civil War many cavalry officers turned to military books to discover how to conduct the economy and operations of their units. Robert Ward's *Animadversions of warre* (1639)—the title means critical observations on war—was highly thought of for its advice on the training and handling of cavalry; but it owed much to what was by far the most popular book, John Cruso's *Militarie Instructions for the Cavallerie*. This was first published in 1632, but was re-printed in 1644 at Cambridge, the heart of the Parliamentarian Eastern Association. Many books were revived and republished to meet the new market generated by the Civil Wars, but such was the dominance of Cruso's book that few others dealt with cavalry. Cruso based his advice upon his own experience in training the Norfolk militia, but also looked back to the works of earlier theorists. Although Cruso's book was written in the year that Gustavus Adolphus died, it contained nothing of the new offensive cavalry tactics practised by the Swedish army.

In 1644 John Vernon published the pamphlet *The young Horse-man, or the honest plain-dealing Cavalier* ('young' meaning inexperienced; and 'Cavalier' indicating a horseman). This was intended to up-date Cruso in the light of two years' experience of the war, rather than to replace his work. In his book *Military Discipline: or the young artilleryman*, William Barriffe stated that he had not touched upon the subject of cavalry because Cruso had said all that there was to say on the subject. Despite running into five editions from 1635, it was not until the last, published in 1661, that a section on cavalry entitled *Some Brief Instructions for the Exercising of the Horse-Troopes* was added by J.B., and this still owed much of its content to the works of Cruso and Ward, which it recommended to its readers.

The Types of Cavalry

Cruso divided cavalry into five types: the lancer, the cuirassier, the harquebusier, the carbine and the dragoon.

The lancer had disappeared from European armies, except for the Scottish border lancers, who rode small horses and were unarmoured. They therefore bore no resemblance to the knightly warriors described by Cruso.

The adoption of the pike as a principal weapon of the infantry in the 16th century had reduced the effectiveness of the cavalry charge, and in response horsemen took to halting outside the reach of the pikemen and firing pistols to try to

A cuirassier gives fire, holding his pistol with the lock upper-most so that the priming powder stays in contact with the sparking wheel. From the frontispiece of John Cruso's *Militarie Instructions for the Cavallerie*, published in 1632 and again in 1644 at the height of the Civil War. (All non-attributed illustrations are from the author's collection)

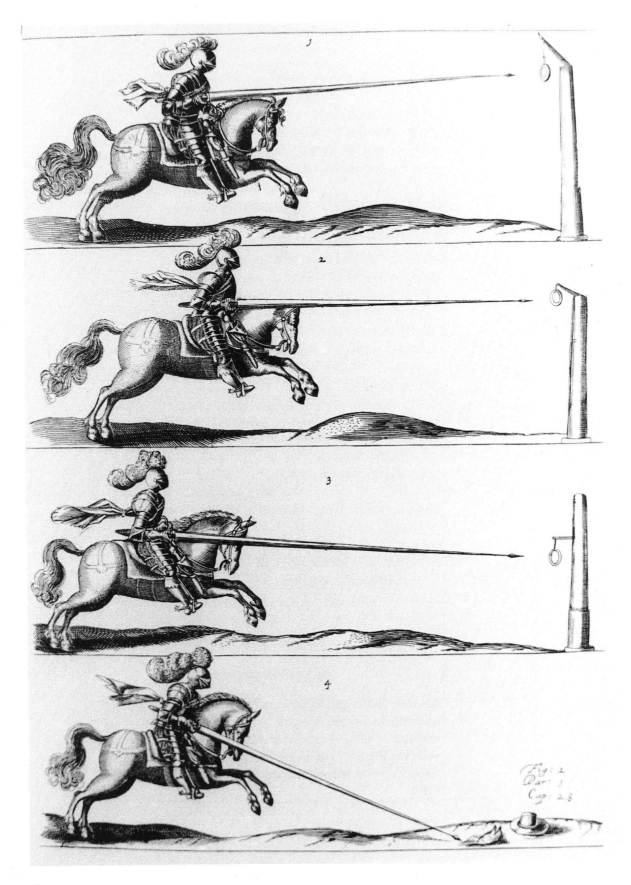

1

2

3

4

Fig: 2
Part: 1
Cap: 28

break their formation. The cuirassier, a heavily armoured horseman equipped with two long-barrelled pistols, a sword and a pole-axe, came to replace the lancer. The dominance of the cuirassier was to be short-lived, for the increased use of the musket, in place of the lighter caliver, meant that the heaviest armour could now be pierced by shot. By 1639 the cuirassier's armour was no longer considered worth the cost and discomfort involved. Sir Edmund Verney, when serving against the Scots, wrote asking to be supplied with lighter armour, 'for it will kill a man to serve in a whole Curass'. The only know cuirassier units to see action in the Civil War were the bodyguard troop of the Earl of Essex, and the regiment of Sir Arthur Haslerigge. These were the only Parliamentarian horse to hold their own against Prince Rupert's Horse in the early stages of the war. Haslerigge's regiment was almost destroyed at the battle of Roundway Down, and the cost of re-equipping the unit as cuirassiers may have proved too great, for a troop from the regiment are later referred to as harquebusiers.

In the 16th and early 17th centuries the fashion for horsemen armed with firearms had led to several new varieties of cavalrymen being created. The rôle of the harquebusier, petronel and carbine was to provide flanking support for the more heavily armoured cuirassier. During the Civil War only the terms carbine and harquebusier survived, and these were used interchangeably to describe the standard cavalryman.

Recruiting

The cavalry regiment that Parliament had intended to send to help quell the Irish rebellion was to have consisted of ten troops each 60 men strong besides officers. At the start of the Civil War both armies formed troops of horse 60 strong, but variations appeared due to the success or failure of individual captains.

Parliament began by appealing to citizens of London to provide a horse and horseman for which they would be paid 2s. 6d. per day. A committee of five nobles sat to appoint officers for

This picture from Cruso shows the training of a lancer to strike at various parts of a horseman's or foot soldier's body. Firearms required little skill or training compared to the lifelong practice needed to master the heavy medieval lance.

every 60 men recruited into a troop by this means. When the Parliamentarian army mustered for the start of its first campaign, orders were issued that only troops with 40 or more men should attend; the remainder were to finish recruiting quickly, or would be broken up to strengthen other troops. At the battle of Edgehill on 23 October 1642 the Parliamentarian troops, which had not yet been properly organised into regiments, were probably close to their notional strengths of 71 men (60 troopers plus officers and office holders). By December 1642 Cromwell was in command of a troop 80 strong, and there was a gradual increase in the size of Parliamentarian horse troops. The average strength of the troops serving with Essex at Tiverton in 1644 was 85 men, although this varied—there were two troops which boasted 100 men, and one which mustered only 44. Parliament's regional armies had more difficulty in maintaining the strength of their regiments: the eight troops of John Frescheville's northern horse regiment averaged only 20 men each during 1644. Many troops of the Eastern Association approached 100 strong and this was the strength set for the New Model Horse (although it was reduced to 80 in the reforms of 1648).

The Royalists raised their army in a more haphazard manner, depending on the generosity of individuals to raise whole troops or regiments. *A True Description of the Discipline of War both of Horse and Foot used in his Maiesties Army . . .* has only this to say of the horse: 'Our horse Troops are to be Carbines, sixty men compleat besides officers'. However, many commissions were issued to raise '500 Horse volunteers', which could not be equally reduced into troops 60 strong. Rather than offering payment for those who could provide a horseman, the king asked his supporters to pay 2s. 6d. per day for three months to support a cavalryman, and relied upon individual captains to recruit the necessary horses and men. Despite a lack or organisation this produced excellent results at the beginning of the war, as the nobility and gentry vied with one another in their generosity to the king's cause. The Marquis of Worcester lent Sir John Byron £5,000 which enabled him to be the first to complete a Royalist regiment of horse. The Earl of Northampton not only paid to support 40 horse but raised a troop of

Cruso illustrates a tactic to be used against an enemy charging 'in full career'. You are to '... devide your body by the half ranks, and so suddenly open to the left and right; so as the enemy passeth through you, and you (facing inward) charge him on the flanks.' Cruso points out that this tactic is the idea of the earlier writer Walhausen, '... but it is very doubtfull. For by this opening to the right and left, you must turn troop, and then make a whole turn again, & so give advantage to your enemie'.

100 gentlemen serving at their own expense. Despite these individual efforts the average strength of Royalist horse troops remained low. Major Legge's troop at Edgehill mustered only 15 men, and the average troop strength at the Aldbourne Chase muster on 10 April 1644 was only 44. Richard Atkyns records the raising of his own troop of Lord Chandos' regiment:

'I raised with such success, that within one month, I mustered 60 men besides officers, and almost all of them well armed; Master Dutton giving me 30 steel backs, breasts and head pieces, and two men and horses completely armed: and this was done upon my duty, without any advance of money, or quarters assigned; wherein every fourth or fifth man was lost ... and about a fortnight after, at the siege of Bristoll, I mustered 80

men besides officers, whereof 20 of them gentlemen that bore arms'.

As the war dragged on the fortunes of the king's officers diminished, but their regiments and troops remained in being, so that it became ever harder to maintain their strength. A single troop could also present a widely fluctuating muster roll, e.g. the troop of Sir Samuel Luke, which fielded the following numbers of troopers during the First Civil War [SP28/127/pt3]:

22 September 1642	=42
27 December 1642	=60
6 March 1643	=56
16 May 1643	=89
20 July 1643	=81
6 November 1643	=75
30 January 1644	=40
20 May 1644	=56
11 July 1644	=71
25 September 1644	=72
25 April 1645	=60

The number of troops in a regiment also varied, with John Vernon quoting seven (each of 72 troopers) and the New Model having a standard of six. In the army of the Eastern Association, Cromwell commanded 14 troops, the Earl of Manchester 11, Charles Fleetwood six, Quartermaster General Vermuyden five and Sir John Norwich a mere three. The most prominent Royalists also maintained large regiments— Prince Rupert's regiment contained ten troops in addition to his 150-strong Lifeguard. In battle, two troops were often combined to form a division or squadron; however, care must be exercised over these terms, as John Vernon divides a single troop into three 'squadrons'.

The field officers of a regiment of horse were a colonel, a lieutenant-colonel (only in the Royalist army and in larger Parliamentarian regiments) and a sergeant major. Each troop consisted of a captain, a lieutenant, a cornet (standard bearer), a quartermaster, three corporals, two trumpeters, a clerk, a saddler, a surgeon, a farrier, and—in theory—60 troopers.

Mounting

Providing horses for the cavalry was to be a major problem throughout the Civil Wars, and several methods were employed to find suitable mounts. Many cavalrymen were recruited with their own horses. If such a horse was killed in action or died of disease a replacement was, in theory, provided by the authorities; but after several years' service it could be difficult to determine to whom a horse belonged. For those who could not provide their own mounts, Parliament sought horses as voluntary contributions from its sympathisers. Each horse was valued, and interest was paid at 8 per cent until the horse, or its estimated value, was returned. In addition the owner was paid 4d. per day hire for his horse, and 2s. 6d. if both horse and rider were provided. As the early enthusiasm for the war waned voluntary contributions became increasingly scarce, and Parliament adapted the system to raise compulsory contributions. On 25 July 1644 Parliament ordered 15 counties to raise 6,500 horse and to deliver them to a list of colonels of horse regiments by given dates.

A popular method of gaining horses was to take them by force from those who supported the enemy. On 1 April 1643 Parliament passed a 'sequestration ordinance' which allowed the horses of 'delinquents' to be seized without compensation. This licensed banditry had a damaging effect both on the discipline of the armies and upon the stability of the community. Stories of bribes paid to protect delinquents and of false accusations by jealous neighbours were common, and the fear of confiscation did nothing to promote the breeding of horseflesh. It is likely that in many cases armies took what horses they needed and justified their actions only if their victims had the influence to complain to King or Parliament.

The most common method of obtaining horses was by direct purchase. At the start of the war Parliament paid its new captains of horse £1,104 mounting money to equip their men with arms and horses. Those who undertook to command a troop were paid £280 mounting money, which was divided so as to give the captain £140, the lieutenant £60, the cornet £50 and the quartermaster £30. The price of horses varied: in July 1644 Cromwell paid £10 each for horses, but during the same year he bought mounts for only £6 at Huntingdon Fair. The New Model Army in 1645 paid £7 10s. for its cavalry mounts and £4 for those of dragoons.

Cruso illustrates 16 motions to load and fire a wheellock pistol. Here the cuirassier returns his rammer after loading powder and ball into the barrel of the pistol. (Dr. S. Bull collection)

13.

Returne your Rammer.

Order your Hammer

Cruso provided four illustrations to show how the loading process of the flintlock differed from that of the wheellock. This motion is 'Order your hammer', in which the iron plate against which the pyrites will spark is positioned over the pan of priming powder. (Dr. S. Bull collection)

Training for Horse and Man

Cruso described how to prepare a cavalry charger for battle: 'When he is at his oats (at a good distance from him) a little powder may be fired, and so near to him by degrees. So may a pistol be fired some distance off, and so nearer: in like manner a drumme or trumpet may be used. The groom may sometime dresse him in armour, and he may be used (now and then) to eat his oats from the drumme head. It will be very usefull sometime to cause a musketier to stand at a convenient distance, and both of you to give fire upon the other, and thereupon to ride up close to him: also to ride him against a compleat armour, so set upon a stake, that he may overthrow it, and trample it under his feet: that so (and by such other means) your horse (finding that he receiveth no hurt) may become bold to approach any object'.

Formations

Since all the horsemen in a troop were armed alike it was not necessary to develop complicated drill movements such as those for changing the relative positions of the musketeers and pikemen within a foot company. In theory a body of horse was drawn up by first deciding how many soldiers should stand one behind another in each file. The number of ranks then depended upon how many files could be filled. At one time a file of eight horsemen had been common, and some theorists said that this should be reduced to five. However, by the beginning of the Civil War the usual number for a file was six, as this could be easily transformed into two files of three, thus increasing the unit's frontage. Fighting with files three deep was criticised as leaving the body 'weak, and not able to endure a Shock'; but when the issue was to be decided by hand-to-hand fighting rather than by firepower, the rear ranks could do little to help, and being outflanked by a wider body of horsemen was a greater danger. Monk and Vernon, both writing in 1644, took horse drawn up in three ranks as normal. The anonymous author of *Some brief Instructions for the exercising of the Horse-Troopes*, published in 1661, said:

'In our late Civil Wars in England... the Chief Commanders in their Exercising of an Infant Troop (such a one as hath been newly raised) did Customarily draw them forth by Ranks, that they might place the best Men and Horse in the Front; the second sort in the Reer, and the third in the middle Rank; and so instead of 8, 6, or 5 in a File, they had but 3: and that for this reason, (besides others that might be given) Because their Front extended larger, and brought more hands to Fight: For a Troop of 64 Horse of 8 in File, brought but 8 in Front; the same Number of 6 deep could not compleat 11 in Front, there wanting 2: And that 5 deep, did not afford 13 in Front, there wanting 1; Whereas this Number, drawn up 3 deep, affords a front of 21, and one over; So that One Troop of 3 in File, was more serviceable, (in bringing hands to Fight) than two Troopes and an half was, that had 8 in File'.

There was disagreement over the distances that should be left between the ranks and files, and this was made worse by the fact that some writers calculated in 'paces' and some in feet and inches. Some said a horse pace was taken as five feet and an infantryman's pace as three feet, but others, such as Monk, measured all paces as three feet. Cruso, writing in 1632, commented that Praissac (*The Art of Warre, or Militarie Discourses*) 'would have the distance between rank and rank (both for the length of the horse, as also for the space between horse and horse) to be six paces, & one pace between file and file. Yet, if we take every pace for five foot (as that is the usuall dimention) by this rule they should be at a verie large distance'. However, when Cruso published his translation of Praissac in 1639, he added a marginal note at this point in the text: 'Paces here are to be understood Steps, and not geometricall paces of 5 foot'.

There was general agreement that six feet, or the length of one horse, should be left between the ranks (i.e. the rear of the front horse and the head of the horse standing behind it). This distance was known as 'open order'. Three feet, known as 'close order', was recommended as the distance for horses standing side by side; but Monk calls this 'order' and recommends that a charge be made in a 'close order' of one and a half feet between horses. With such confusion amongst the theorists, the cavalry general could find each of his units employing different formations depending upon which book their officers had read. Only the experience of war, or a strong-minded commander, could impose uniformity of drill on an army.

Manoeuvres

Having formed his troop into ranks and files the captain then moved on to manoeuvres. John Vernon in *The Young Horse-man* described them:

'The Motions for the Cavalrie are of foure kinds, as Facings, Doublings, Countermarchings, and Wheelings: the use of Facings is to make the Troop perfect, to be sodainly prepared for a Charge on either Flank or Reare, Doublings of Ranks or by half Files, or by Bringers up, serveth to strengthen the Front, Doubling the Files serveth to strengthen the Flanks, Countermarching serveth to reduce the File-leaders into the place of the Bringers up, that so the best men may

A harquebusier gives fire with a wheellock carbine which is carried on a narrow carbine belt. He has his bullet pouch and powder flask suspended from a waist belt.

Printed by the Printers to the University of Cambridge

be ready to receive the charge of the Enemy in the Reare: the use of Wheelings is to bring the Front which commonly consists of best and ablest men to receive the Charge of the Enemy on either Flank or Reare, and also unexpected to Charge the Enemy on either Flanke or Reare.'

Facings were carried out by the simple expedient of each man turning his horse to the left or right at the same time. When wheeling, the front corner man of the body stood still while the rest of the front rank moved in an arc around him. The other ranks followed the man to their front.

Doublings were executed in two ways. For instance, the order 'Ranks, to the right double' was intended to result in a body with twice as many men in each rank as there were before: the second, fourth and sixth ranks would move into the gaps between the horsemen in the first, third and fifth ranks respectively. The second method was for the fourth rank, known as the half file leaders, to lead the fifth and sixth ranks into the gaps between the first three ranks.

Countermarching was a difficult and dangerous manoeuvre to execute, as the body of horse could easily become disordered. The aim was to have the formation turn to face in the opposite direction, but with the original front rank still in the front. The front rank turned to the left or right as ordered and marched down the intervals between the files, the horseman behind riding up to the spot where the first had turned and following him down between the files. In this way the body marched through itself. This was known as the 'Choraean countermarch', and there were variants named after the Macedonians and Lacedemonians. It is doubtful if the countermarch was ever used in the field, as it was difficult to execute with infantry let alone with horsemen, where an unruly mount could wreck a whole formation.

Cavalry Uniforms and Equipment

Although we can identify the coat colours of many infantry regiments from warrants and recorded sightings, we have little reliable evidence for the

A spanner for setting the mechanism of a wheellock pistol. Cruso describes it thus: 'For the more speedy lading of the pistoll, and avoiding the trouble of carrying either flasque or touchbox, there is a late invented fashion of spanner or key, which contains six charges of powder.' (National Army Museum)

The Dutch and Spanish horse exchange volleys of pistol shot at the battle of Niueport in 1600. Pistols were fired at short range to achieve maximum penetration of the enemy's armour.

clothing issued to cavalry. Some accounts have survived, such as that of Sir Thomas Dallison, who obtained 300 or 400 yards of red cloth to make cloaks for Prince Rupert's Horse; and of a quartermaster of the Earl of Denbigh's Horse, who obtained eight and a half yards of grey cloth. Most Civil War officers regarded any cloth that they could obtain as suitable to clothe their soldiers, regardless of its colour, and the above examples do not prove that uniform was worn by cavalry. Personal retinues of officers were sometimes dressed in uniform outfits, but this was common before the war, and involved only a handful of servants.

The New Model Army, like earlier Parliamentary armies, issued its foot soldiers with coats and breeches, and one warrant specifies that such coats are only for foot soldiers. During its later campaigns the New Model issued cloaks to its horsemen, and it may be that these were the standard alternative to coats for horse troopers throughout the war. Monk assumes that the cavalryman will wear a doublet with hooks and eyes

to support his breeches, and some have suggested that buff coats were so universal that uniform clothing was unnecessary.

With uniforms in doubt, the use of a scarf or sash to show allegiance was even more important. John Vernon makes it clear that horsemen, but not common foot soldiers wore sashes:

'Every horseman must weare a skarfe of his Generalls Colours, and leave it off neither in his quarters nor out of his quarters, it being an ornament unto him: besides it will cause him to forbeare many unfitting actions, as being thereby distinguished from the vulgar or common souldiour, it is likewise a good and visible mark in time of battell to know one another'.

In the early part of the war the Royalists wore red or crimson sashes and Parliamentarians orange, the colour of the Earl of Essex. Other colours were worn by soldiers in regional armies according to the choice of their commanders. In September 1642 troopers were given 10s. each to buy a 'scarfe', which was a great deal of money considering that a superior quality horseman's sword cost only 8s. at that time. It may be that the sash was so important because cavalrymen did not wear a uniform coat.

Weapons and Armour

In 1644 John Vernon described the arming of the harquebusier as follows: 'His defensive Arms, as only an open Caske or Head-peece, a back and breast with buffe coat under his armes; his offensive Armes are a good Harquebus, [or] a Carbine hanging on his right side in a belt by a sweble, a flask and Carthareg case, and spanner, and good firelock pistols in houlsters. At his saddle a good stiffe sword sharp pointed, and a good poll-axe in his hand, a good tall horse of fifteen handfulls high, strong and nimble, with false raines to your bridle made of an Iron Chain'.

During the same year Monk wrote that the defensive arms of the horseman were: 'An Head-piece with three small iron Bars to defend the Face, Back, and Breast; all three Pistol-proof: a Gauntlet for his left hand, or a good long Buff Glove. A Girdle of double Buff about eight inches broad, which is to be worn under the skirts of his Doublet'.

These passages may be compared with a selection of the items issued to the cavalrymen of the New Model Army in 1645/46:

'Two hundred potts with three barres English at VIIs a peece'.

'One hundred Troope sadles with the furniture and Stran Bitts at sixteene shillings & sixpence'.

'59 Carbines full bore & proofe with Swivells at XIIs IXd a peece.

'820 Carbine belts of good leather & strong buckles according to the patterne at 8d a peece & for 500 Cartridge Girdles at 2s. 8d. a dosen'.

'Two hundred payre of snaphaunce pistolls full bore & proofe with holsters of calveskins inside & outside well sewed & liquored at XXs IIIId a payre.'

'Two hundred Armes backs brests and potts at 20s per suite.'

'Swords & Belts—3200—The Mr Wardens & Company of Cutlers in London att 5s per sword

Detail of Sprigge's map of the Parliamentarian right flank at the battle of Naseby in 1645. The figures of horsemen are representative: each block consisted of three troops. The three-rank formation is clearly shown, as is the tactic of leaving spaces between the troops to allow other bodies to move up in support or fall back in retreat.

& belt whereof 200 horsemens swords.'

The Royalists have often been portrayed as wearing no armour, but this can be disproved by warrants and receipts, such as that of 14 December 1642:

'*Charles R*

Our Will and Pleasure is, That you deliuer to the Bearer hereof Captaine Gerard Croker Fourty and foure Horse Armes; And for soe doeing this shall bee your Warrant. Giuen at Our Court att Oxford this 14th of December 1642.

To the Officers of Our Magazyne

Received out of his Mats Stores for the use of my Troop viz.

Backs 33
Breasts 33
Potts 33
Vambraces one pre. Gauntletts. 2.
Holdsters ....13 pre.
Gorgetts 25

Gerard Croker'

This demonstrates that even very early in the war the Royalists both intended to have and actually received armour for their cavalry.

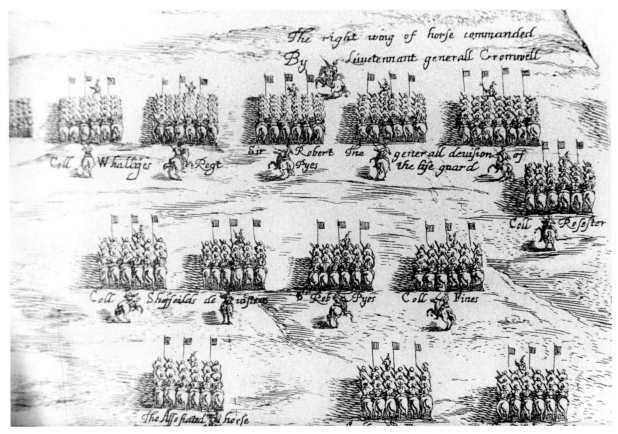

However, the fact that only 33 sets of 'Armes' were supplied when 44 were requested, as well as the deficiencies in 'Gorgetts' and holsters, indicates that equipment was in short supply.

The Carbine

Although the majority of the cavalrymen of the Civil War were known as 'harquebusiers' rather than 'carbines', the weapon they carried was described as a carbine. The exact nature of the firearm that the light cavalryman should carry had been the subject of debate for most of the century, and each theorist had his own proposals to make. Markham in 1625 suggested that 'He shal have an Hargobus of three foot three inches long, and the bore of twentie Bullets in the pound'. Cruso in 1632 advocated a lighter, shorter weapon: 'He must have the harquebusse of two foot and a half long (the bore of 17 bullets in the pound rolling in)'. Robert Ward in 1639 was content to follow Cruso: 'Their Harquebuzes are to be two foote and a halfe in length, their bores of seventeene bullets to the pound'. With some experience of war Monk in 1644 put forward the need for a more powerful firearm: 'A Carbine, or a Musquet-barrel of the length of a Carbine-barrel, well stockt with a Snapance: the which I hold to be much better then a Carbine for Service'.

The government's specification for a carbine in 1630 was for a barrel length of two and a half feet with a bore of 24 bullets 'rolling'. In 1638 a snaphaunce carbine cost £1 'with belts, swivells, worms and skowrers and arming the stock to be made up 2 ft 6 in long and of the bore of 24 bullets to the pound rowelling'. Surviving examples of carbines preserved at Littlecote House, which may have belonged to Alexander Popham's Parliamentarian troopers, have barrels 21½ in. long and a bore (.82 in.) slightly larger than that of a standard musket (.8 in.).

C. H. Firth (*Cromwell's Army*, 1901) was under the impression that carbines were not issued to the horse of the Eastern Association or to that of the New Model. The New Model contracts make it clear that carbines were issued, although they do not give any description as to bore or length of barrel.

Despite the fact that the Royalists favoured the

The Religious successfull and truly Valliant Lieutenant Generall Cromwell

Oliver Cromwell is due his place in history as a notable commander of cavalry. His firm religious beliefs led him to carefully select the officers and troopers of his 14 troop regiments while his influence in the peaceful and prosperous counties of East Anglia gave him the resources to keep them in pay. (D. Carter collection)

sword above the firearm in their cavalry tactics, there is clear evidence among the surviving ordnance papers that they tried to equip their cavalrymen with carbines. A receipt dated 10 December 1642 indicates that in the early days of the war such items were in short supply:

'Oxford, Received out of his Mats Stores for the use of Collonell Astons Regimt of Horse.

Carabines with Firelocks	2
Carabines wanting locks	4
Swordes wanting scaberds	18
Sworde blades	3 (deleted)
Belts for Carbines	13
Sworde Belts	6'

The situation evidently improved, for carbine ammunition was delivered as frequently as that for pistols throughout the war.

The Pistol

The pistols used during the Civil Wars can be divided between those fitted with wheellocks and those with various forms of flintlock. The wheel-lock was a complicated mechanism, and prone to jamming if kept 'spanned' ready for firing for a long time. The flintlock was simpler, and in 1639 a pair of pistols fitted with snaphance locks cost £2 5s. as against £3 for a pair using wheellocks. Although the wheellock retained its popularity on the Continent for some years, the flintlock was favoured by English gunsmiths. This may have led to a distinction between the pistols used by the two sides, for with control of London Parliament had many gunsmiths to call upon. Although some pistols were produced in Royalist-held areas like Sheffield, many of their weapons were imported from the Continent. That these pistols were wheellocks is demonstrated by the inclusion of spanners to wind up their mechanisms in warrants such as that for 10 November 1643: 'To issue out of his Mats magazine twenty Case of pistolls with Houlsters and spanners, and twenty Carabynes ... for the Arminge of the Regimt of Horse of Sr Arthur Aston.

Pistolls with Hollsters ....20 payre
Spanners 30
Carabynes 20
Firestones 20

Many of these weapons were imported from Holland, but their quality was poor. A typical order of 8 December 1643, was for 6,000 muskets at 21s. each, 1,000 carbines at 31s. and 1,000 pistols at 51s. per pair.

Surviving examples of 'munition' quality pistols show a low standard of workmanship in both lock and stock, and many may have been produced by local craftsmen. The Council of War held in 1630 specified that pistols should have barrels 18 in. long, but records exist of imported pistols with barrels 26 in. in length (which proved too long to fit into English holsters), while the post-Restoration standard was for barrels of 14 inches. Whatever the length of barrel the pistol was used at very close range, both because of its inaccuracy and its small bore: to have any hope of penetrating the armour of an enemy a pistol had to be almost touching its target. Richard Atkyns records his engagement with the fully armoured Sir Arthur Haslerigge at Roundway Down:

'He discharged his carbine first, but at a distance not to hurt us, and afterwards one of his

William Cavendish, Duke of Newcastle (1592–1676) commanded the Royalists in northern England, and during 1643 made heavy work of defeating a small Parliamentarian army. In 1644 he faced the invading Scots, and his tardiness in joining Prince Rupert before Marston Moor may have cost the Royalists victory. After the battle he fled to the Continent, where he wrote a book on horsemanship which remains his chief claim to fame. (D. Carter collection)

pistols, before I came up to him, and missed with both: I then immediately struck into him, and touched him before I discharged mine; and I'm sure I hit him, for he staggered, and presently wheeled off from his party and ran. I came up to him, and discharged the other pistol at him, and I'm sure I hit his head, for I touched it before I gave fire.'

Cartridges and Powder Flasks

The idea of carrying a single charge of powder in a paper cartridge was not new in the Civil War. Sir John Smythe, in his *Instructions, Observations, and Orders Mylitarie* published in 1595, recommended that cavalrymen: 'have at their saddle pommels very good single pistolles, in good cases well and firmelie sette at their saddles ... with a Cartage boxe of Iron of 7 or 8 cartages fast set upon everie pistoll case'.

John Vernon includes a cartridge case as well as a flask in his list of necessary equipment for a harquebusier, and describes their use: 'Now if you use Cartrages, you will shall finde in your Carttreg case a turned wooden pin which you must take, having cut lengths of white paper something broader then the pin is in length, and roule the paper on the pin, then twist one end of the paper, and fill it almost full of powder, then put the bullet on the top of the powder, twisting that end also, then put it into your Carttreg case'.

However, Vernon advocates the use of the flask, saying: 'Use a flask rather than a horne or Cartheages for your charge is quicker provide, and if you provided Carteages, they are subject with the trotting of your Horse to lose all the powder out of them'.

Despite this criticism the New Model accounts describe the purchase of 2,200 'Cartridges' and 700 Cartridge Girdles, one contract specifying: '1,200 Cartridges the boxes of stronge plate covered with black leather 700 of them halfe round & the other 500 double at Xd'.

It has been claimed that these cartridge boxes were for issue to Dragoons, and resembled the large rectangular cartridge 'belly boxes' issued to some grenadiers in the 18th century. However, the numbers produced conform to the numbers of carbines and carbine belts ordered on the same day, and it is likely that they were intended for use by cavalrymen. Their appearance and design remains unknown, but they may have resembled the 'patrons' used in the 16th century; these were 'half round' metal cartridge boxes containing a wooden former which was drilled to accommodate six cartridges.

The cartridge was neither new nor revolutionary at the time of the Civil War, and was regarded as a poor substitute for other means of containing and measuring gunpowder.

Buff Coats

The buff coat developed from the arming doublet which was worn under full body armour. This was made of leather with sections of ring-mail where the joints in the armour failed to offer protection, and often had straps and ties for securing the separate pieces of armour. It offered some protection to the body and clothing of the wearer, preventing the edges of the metal rubbing and tearing. As the wearing of armour declined the buff coat came to be valued for the protection that it could offer in its own right. Monk recommends

PRINCE RUPERT.

Prince Rupert was more than an inspiring leader; despite his youth he had wide experience of continental warfare, and was a keen student of military theory. His daring and skill gave victory to the Royalist horse in most of the early battles of the Civil Wars. (D. Carter collection)

a girdle of buff to be worn below the back and breastplates rather than underneath them; these are clearly to protect the legs from sword cuts rather than as an underlining to the armour. Contemporary pictures of European soldiers show sleeveless buff coats cut short, which are worn only as padding under armour, and this idea was also adapted by having leather linings fixed into individual pieces of armour.

Buff coats came in many patterns and in varying thicknesses and qualities. John Turbervill wrote of buff coats in September 1640 that there was 'not a good one to be gotten under £10, a very poor one for five or six pounds'. However, we may take it that Turbervill's poor buff coat was much superior to those issued to common soldiers, for in 1647 Colonel Thorpe paid only 30s. each for three buff coats [SP28/135]; and in 1642 Sir Samuel Luke paid £58 15s. 4d. for buff coats for his harquebusiers [SP28/127]. Unfortunately,

Luke does not tell us how many buff coats his money bought, but the same accounts indicate that he was trying to equip 64 men. It is difficult to speculate what a 30s. buff coat might have been like, for the troopers' buff coats preserved at Littlecote are well made, of thick leather and fully sleeved, while an example in the National Army Museum is crudely made and lacks sleeves. It is worth remembering that a New Model cavalryman's helmet and back and breast cost only 20s. making even a cheap buff coat an expensive addition.

Cavalry in Battle

Civil War cavalry tactics were derived from the experience of soldiers who had served in the Dutch and Swedish armies. However, as the two sides followed separate trends, we must examine them individually.

The Royalists

From the earliest days of the Civil War the tactics employed by the Royalist Horse were determined by Prince Rupert. An experienced commander during the European wars, Rupert had also made a study of military textbooks; he was therefore up to date in his ideas, and introduced the latest shock tactics to the Royalist army. At Edgehill he formed both wings of the Royal Horse in files three deep, and gave instructions that they should 'March as close as possible, keeping their ranks with sword in hand, to receive the enemy's shot without firing either carbine or pistol till we broke in amongst the enemy, and then to make use of our firearms as need should require' [Bulstrode's Memoirs].

This was to be the basis of Royal cavalry tactics throughout the Civil Wars. Rupert consistently sought to take the initiative and carry the charge to his enemy, without pause for the use of firearms. Against irresolute or inexperienced opponents these tactics were almost always successful, and in the early years of the war it came to be accepted that no Parliamentarian horse could stand against the charge of Rupert's cavalry.

Rupert employed the tactic of placing bodies of musketeers amongst his horsemen. These 'commanded musketeers' were fulfilling the rôle of dragoons in providing firepower to break up an enemy formation prior to the charge of their own horse. The Parliamentary armies tried this tactic at Edgehill, but with such little success that they did not repeat the experiment. Their cavalry 'Did discharge their long pieces [i.e. carbines] afar off

Figures from Cruso show two ways in which the carbine was carried: hanging below the right arm on the march, and supported on the right thigh when about to go into action or passing through a town.

and without distance, [i.e. out of effective range] and immediately thereafter wheeled all about and ran disorderly, leaving the Musqueteers to be cut in pieces by the enemy.'

The Parliamentarians

The Royalists were fortunate to find a cavalry leader of note to provide them with successful tactics at the outset of the war. The Parliamentarians had to learn by their mistakes at the cost of several reverses in battle. Early tactics were based on the teachings of the Dutch army which had been the dominant force at the start of the century. They relied upon firepower to break up an enemy formation. When attacking, the procedure was to send one rank at a time forward to fire its carbines and pistols at the enemy until sufficient casualties and disruption amongst his ranks had been caused for the rest of the body to charge home. Given that the basic Royalist tactic was to initiate a charge at the first possible moment, the Parliamentarians had little opportunity to use this slow and leisurely form of attack.

Detail from a picture of the battle of Turnhoult in 1600 between the Spanish, and the Dutch and their English allies. The Dutch cuirassiers are drawn up in formation nine deep and have 61 men in each troop. They are therefore much the same size as the standard troop in both the Royalist and Parliamentarian armies.

In defence, the enemy's charge was received at the stand, in the hope that weight of fire would break up the attack and open the way for a successful countercharge. This tactic has often been scorned as ineffective but, as with so much of the Dutch school of tactics, its success depended upon the training and steadfastness of the soldiers. The tactic could work if fire was reserved until the proper moment. '*A Letter Purporting the True Relation of the Skirmish at Worcester*' tells this story of Nathaniel Fiennes' Parliamentarian troopers at Powick Bridge:

'We let them come up very near that their horses' noses almost touched those of our front rank before ours gave fire, and then [our men] gave fire, and very well to my thinking, with their carbines, after [which we] fell in with good hope to have broken them (being pretty well shattered

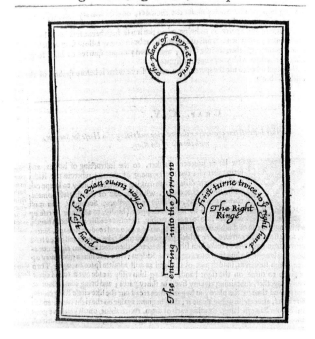

Robert Ward advises the use of the ring to teach a horse to turn properly on the rider's command. A series of exercises in the ring taught the horse to make tight turns in battle.

with the first charge of [our] carbines). But of a sudden we found all the troops on both sides of us melted away, and our rear being carried away with them'.

Reliance upon Dutch military theories also led to the Parliamentarians drawing up their horse in files six deep, unlike the Royalists who followed the Swedish practice of forming files three deep. By 1644 the Parliamentary horse had adopted the three deep formation, but still relied upon firearms to a greater extent than the Royalists. John Vernon in *The young Horse-man . . .* of 1644 gives this advice on how a charge should be conducted:

'All the Troops are to be drawn up into battalia, each being not above three deepe, likewise each troop must be at least a hundred paces distance behind each other for the better avoiding of disorder, those troops that are to give the first charge being drawn up into battail as before, are to be at their close order, every left hand mans right knee must be close locked under his right hand mans left ham, as hath bin shown before. In this order they are to advance toward

the Enemy with an easy pace, firing their Carbines at a convenient distance, always aiming at their Enemies brest or lower, because that powder is of an elevating nature, then drawing neere the Enemy, they are with their right hands to take forth one of their Pistols out of their houlsters, and holding the lock uppermost firing as before, always reserving one Pistol ready charged, spann'd and primed in your houlsters, in case of a retreat as I have shown before, having thus fired the troops are to charge the Enemy in full career, but in good order with their swords fastned with a Riband or the like unto their wrists, for fear of losing out of their hand, if they should chance to misse their blow, placing the pomel on their thigh, keeping still in their close order, locked as before'.

The essential difference between the tactics described above and those employed by the Parliamentarians in the early stages of the war was that the use of firearms was only a prelude to the charge. It may be that the use of firearms caused the charge of the Parliamentarians to be executed at a slower and more controlled pace than that of the Royalist horse. However 'a good trot' was the recommended pace for a charge, and a steady controlled approach could be of advantage.

Grand Tactics

A general could exercise very little control over his cavalry once they had been launched into a charge. With the horse invariably divided on to the wings of a central battle of foot units, the main area in which a commander could influence the cavalry battle was in the placing of his formations and in the deployment of his reserve. *Brief Instructions . . .* laid down some rules:

'Many times the Horse Troopes are divided into Six Battaliaes, whereof Three placed upon one Wing, and three upon the other; As suppose the Number to be 4,000 Horse, the two foremost Battels or Divisions upon each wing, are to consist of 1,000; the two Second Battels of 500 each; and the two last or Reer, to consist of 300 each; the other 400 to be placed where they may be ready to perform any sudden Command of the General: There ought to be a good distance betwixt each of these Battels'.

Monk advises that a body of horse should be broken up into divisions to increase the flexibility of the attack. He says that a body of 300 horse should be split into five divisions of 60 troopers. They can then attack all together, or with some divisions held in reserve to follow up and complete a charge. Having a large number of divisions to handle increased the dangers of a general failing to keep control of his command. The result of this is shown by the collapse of Commissary General Ireton's wing of the New Model Army at Naseby:

'Upon that the Enemy advanced again, whereupon our Left wing sounded a Charge, and fell upon them: The three right hand Divisions of our Left wing made the first onset, and those Divisions of the enemy opposite to them, received the Charge; the two left hand Divisions of the Left wing did not advance equally, but being more backward, the opposite Division of the Enemy advanced upon them. Of the three right hand Divisions (before mentioned) which advanced, the middlemost charged not home, the other two coming to a close Charge, routed the two opposite Divisions of the Enemy, (And the Commissary Generall seeing one of the enemies Brigades of Foot on his right hand, pressing sore upon our Foot, commanded the Division that was with him, to charge that Body of Foot, and for their better encouragement, he himself with great resolution fell in amongst the Musquetiers. . . . That Division of the enemies which was between, which the other Division of ours should have charged, was carried away in the disorder of the other two; the one of those right hand Divisions of our Left wing that did rout the front of the enemy, charged the Reserve too, and broke them, the other Reserves of the enemy came on, and broke those Divisions of ours that charged them; the Divisions of the left hand of the right wing were likewise overborn, having much disadvantage, by reason of pits of water, and other pieces of ditches that they expected not, which hindred them in their order to Charge.' [*Anglia Rediviva*, Joshua Sprigge. p37.]

Cromwell gives a good example of how, at Gainsborough, his main force having routed part of the enemy, he maintained his advantage by keeping part of his force as a reserve under his personal control:

'I perceiving this body which was the [Royalist] Reserve standing still unbroken, kept back my Major, Whalley, from the chase; and

with my own troop and the other of my regiment, in all being three troops, we got into a body. In this Reserve stood General Cavendish; who one while faced me, another while faced four of the Lincoln troops which was all of ours that stood upon the place, the rest being engaged in the chase. At last General Cavendish charged the Lincolneers, and routed them. Immediately I fell on his rear with my three troops; which did so astonish him, that he did give over the chase, and

Ward provides details of formation for horse troops. Here he gives the formation to be used on the march and the positions that the officers are to take in a troop 120 men strong.

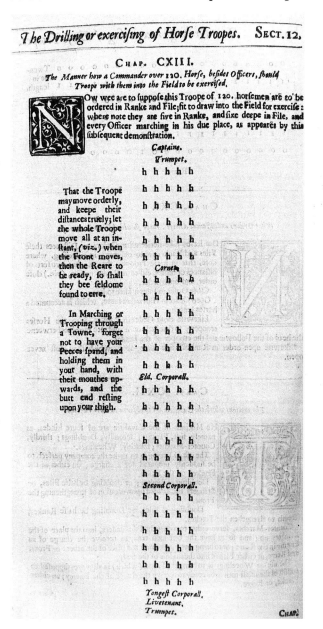

The Drilling or exercising of Horse Troopes. SECT. 12.

CHAP. CXIII.

The Manner how a Commander over 120. Horse, besides Officers, should Troope with them into the Field to be exercised.

NOw wee are to suppose this Troope of 120. horsemen are to be ordered in Ranke and File; fit to draw into the Field for exercise: where note they are five in Ranke, and sixe deepe in File, and every Officer marching in his due place, as appeares by this subsequent demonstration.

would fain have delivered himself from me'.

Unlike Cromwell, Ireton allowed himself to become involved in the fighting rather than staying back with the reserve. When the critical moment came and his own forces were routed, Cromwell was in a position to counterattack and Ireton was not.

Dragoons

The Theorists

Theorists did not have a great deal to say about the dragoon. Since he did not fight on horseback there was no need for complicated evolutions to bring him into the correct battle formation. When he dismounted he became an infantryman, and most writers referred to a book on foot drill at this point. Cruso devoted only nine lines to the dragoon; but Gervase Markham, in *The Soldier's Accidence* of 1635, said:

'The last sort of which our Horse troopes are compounded, are called Dragons, which are a kinde of footman on Horsebacke, and doe now indeed succeed the light Horsemen, and are of singular use in all the actions of Warre, their Armes defensive are an open headpeece, with cheeks, and a good buffe coat, with deepe skirts; and for offensive arms, they have a fayre Dragon fitted with an Iron worke to be carried in a Belt of leather, which is buckled over the right shoulder, and under the left arme, having a Turnell of Iron with a ring through which the peece runneth up and downe; and these Dragons are short peeces of 16 inches the Barrell, and full musket bore, with firelocks or snap-haunces: also a belt, with a Flaske, pryming-boxe, key, and bullet-bag, and a good sword'.

Robert Ward, in *Animadversions of Warre* (1639), reiterated Cruso's thoughts in a section entitled *How the Dragoones ought to arme and demeane themselves*: 'The Dragoones are no lese than a foote company, consisting of Pikes and Muskets, only for their quicker expedition they are mounted upon horses. they are of greate use for the guarding of passages and fordes, in regard of their swiftnesse they may prevent the enemies foote, and gaine places of advantage to hinder their passage.

'Their Pikes are to have thongs of leather about the middle of them, for the easier carriage of them.

'The Muskets are to have a broad strong belt fastened to the stocke of them, well neere from one end to the other, whereby he hangs it upon his backe when he rideth, holding his match and bridle in his left hand: any horse if he be swifte will performe this service, in regard they alight and doe their service a foote; so that when tenne men alight, the eleventh holdeth their horses, so that to every troope of 120 there is 132 men allowed'.

Experience of battle led to new ideas about the dragoon. The pike-armed dragoon was never adopted in England, and it was quickly realised that a matchlock was impracticable on horseback.

Having formed his troop into a block of six ranks by 20 files, Ward takes them through some changes of formation. Shown here are (top) reducing the number of ranks by the fourth, fifth and sixth ranks marching into the gaps between the first three ranks; (centre) the same achieved by the sixth rank leading the others forward; bottom) the body turning about by the first rank leading the others down the files.

Markham's dragoon armed with a 16 in. barrel firelock would have been at a great disadvantage against a musketeer armed with a full-size musket. By 1644 George Monk, writing his *Observations upon Military and Political Affairs* as a prisoner in the Tower of London, described the offensive arms of the dragoon as: 'A musquet, or a good Snapance to a Musquet Barrel; the which I hold much better for Dragoon-Service, being upon occasion they may be able to make use of their Snapances on Horse-back, and upon any Service in night they may go undiscovered. He must have also a belt to hang his Musquet in, with a pair of Bandaliers and a good long Tuck, with a Belt. And all your Dragoons ought to have Swine-feathers.'

With his experience of the wars in Ireland, Monk advocated a dragoon armed with a full bore musket. Like the typical musketeer, Monk's dragoon was to carry his powder charges in a bandolier of between 12 and 15 'boxes'—wooden tubes covered in leather, each made to hold enough powder for a single shot. Monk also suggested the use of 'Swine', or 'Swedish feathers': these were poles fitted with pike heads at both ends. One end was thrust into the ground so that the protruding end would fend off enemy cavalry. Monk was keen that his soldiers should have hatchets to cut wood to prevent them breaking their cheap swords.

As theorists had laid so much emphasis on the fact that the dragoons performed their service on foot, it is strange that Monk wrote of them firing from horseback; however, he was not the only soldier writing during the Civil War to mention this. In June 1644 Captain Nathaniell Burt published a broadside on the subject of dragoons entitled *Militarie Instructions, Or the Souldier Tried, for the use of the Dragon*. Burt begins by referring the reader to certain sections of Cruso's *Militarie Instructions for the Cavallerie* and Barriffe's *Young Artillerie Man* which he says will serve for the dragoon on horse and foot. He continues:

For the exercise of the Dragoone, firing on horseback, I will recite somewhat, I have seen, though in a more confused manner and way, and give some directions to performe the same.

'Suppose the enemy retreating, and their horse facing while they draw off their great guns, and baggage, marching away with the Infantry, they

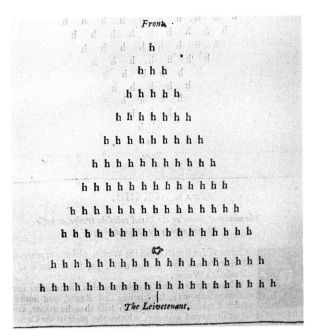

Like most authors of the time Ward looked back to the history of the Romans and Greeks to find the perfect military formation. Here he reproduces a wedge used by the cavalry of Alexander the Great.

losing ground, retreat entire, together, with their Cornets on the head of their Troups, they being on a hill, having a deep and dangerous dale, to friend, fit to lay Ambuscadoes in, besides the night approaching to help them, etc. Here Dragoones may do better service, firing on horse-back, then the Curasier, the way being dubitable, & by advancing slowly after them, following them about musket shot, the curasier being withing such distance as is needful, to relive them, if that the enemy should seem to charge, or attempt it: for the better performance thereof, they are to fire by introduction, on horse-back; which is a passing through, or between the Files, the files being at open Order: the first rank having given fire, by the Commanders direction, let the bringer-up passe through the Files, which is commonly to the left, placing themselves before their Leaders, in the front, and then giving fire, the rest of the Ranks acting the same successively, till such time as they shall receive Order to the contrary, or to close their Files.

'Secondly, a party of Dragoons may fire retreating, on horse-back, and do good execution, they riding such a pace, as their occasion requireth, or the ground will permit, the last rank sometimes

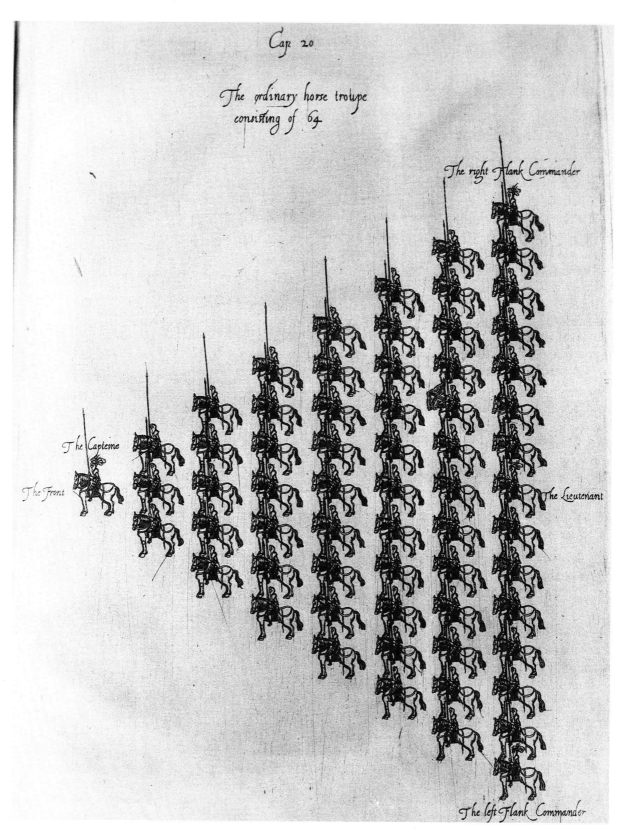

Cap 20

The ordinary horse troupe consisting of 64

The right Flank Commander

The Capteine

The Front

The Lieutenant

The left Flank Commander

From Ward's formation we move to John Bingham's illustration of the wedge, taken from *The Tactiks of Aelian* printed in 1616. Despite its popularity with military theorists, the wedge was probably never used during contemporary wars.

facing about, and firing upon the enemie, then wheeling off to the right, or left as the ground best affords.'

Sir James Turner, writing in 1670, could view the Civil Wars with the benefit of hindsight. In his book *Pallas Armata* he writes: 'Dragoons then go not only before to guard Passes (as some imagine) but to fight in open Field; for if an Enemy rencounter with a Cavalry in a champaign or open Heath, the Dragoons are obliged to alight, and mix themselves with the Squads of Horse, as they shall be commanded; and their continuate Firing, before the Horse come to the charge, will no doubt, be very hurtful to the Enemy: If the encounter be in a closed Countrey, they serve well to line Hedges, and possess Enclosures. . . .'

Turner emphasised that the service of the dragoon was on foot, but said that they should be taught to give fire on horseback so that they could hold off an enemy until they could retire to some defensible position. Turner advised that dragoons on foot should fire in one of the three ways used by musketeers: first, by introduction, where the rear rank marches up the files to the front of the body and gives fire; second, by extroduction, where the front rank fires and retires to the back of the body; and third, by doubling the half files to bring six ranks into three, and then firing all together with the front man kneeling, the second stooping and the third standing.

Dragoons in the Civil War

In the day-to-day conduct of the Civil War the dragoon proved to be the most useful of all soldiers. The most serious problem faced by a garrison commander was how to keep the surrounding area under his control and the flow of levied money and supplies coming in to support his soldiers. Cheap to raise and equip, the dragoon could use his superior mobility to scour friendly countryside for supplies and to make forays into enemy-held territory.

When attached to a field army the dragoon would again be sent to find forage, but he would also be expected to play a rôle as scout for the army. Dragoons were often placed on picket duty, guarding the army in camp, making use of their firelocks—which did not require a constantly burning match as did the matchlock musket.

Okey, the commander of the dragoon regiment in the New Model Army, found that his men were called upon to perform all the picket duties during the 1645 campaign, despite the fact that the cavalry were then armed with carbines.

With their inferior supply system the Royalists found it difficult to provide their dragoons with muskets fitted with snaphances. A warrant of 21 November 1642 states: 'To furnish Coll: Ed: Grey for his Redgiment of Dragoners with twelve Bundells of Match fower Barrells of powder tow barrells of Musket Bullet & tow of Carrabine'.

This indicates that the muskets being used were matchlocks and that carbines were also pressed into service. Just under a month later, on 14 December 1642, the King's Council of War at Oxford took matters in hand and ordered that workmen should be employed to make up muskets for dragoons. It was specified that these muskets were to be only three feet long. Royalist dragoons must have been eager to replace their matchlocks with the more useful snaphances, and there is a record of the issue to Prince Rupert's Dragoons of 30 snaphances on 5 November 1644. However, it is not clear if the regiment had had such weapons previously, or if the dragoons of the king's nephew received preferential treatment.

Dragoons in battle

The dragoon had no place in the military theorist's battle plan, and was most often given the task of supporting the cavalry by firing from the flanks. On occasion dragoons would be used to clear the way for the main attack of the cavalry by capturing some obstacle such as a ditch or hedge, as did Frazer's Scottish Dragoons at Marston Moor. Their superior mobility gave them an advantage over musketeers; but, lacking the support of pikemen, they could only stand against horse or foot if they had the advantage of terrain or cover. Richard Atkyns in his *Vindication* gives two examples of dragoons in action, seen from the viewpoint of an enemy cavalry officer. Of the action at Chewton on 10 June 1643 Atkyns reports:

'When we came within 20 score of the enemy, we found about 200 dragoons half musket shot before a regiment of horse of theirs in two divisions, both in order to receive us. At this punctilio of time, from as clear a sunshine day as could be

The Right Valiant and
Expert Commander Sr
William Waller Kt etc

W. Riddiard Excudit

Sir William Waller commanded the main Parliamentarian armies in south-west England. Although a notable tactician Waller was hampered by a lack of support from the counties of the Southern Association. Despite many disadvantages he triumphed at Cheriton, and halted the tide of Royalist victory at a critical stage in the war. (D. Carter collection)

seen, there fell a sudden mist, that we could not see ten yards off, but we still marched on; the dragoons amazed with the mist, hearing our horse come on; gave us a volley of shot out of distance, and disordered not one man of us, and before we came up to them, they took horse and away they run, and in the mist immediately vanished. We had then the less work to do, but still we had enough; for there were 6 troops of horse in 2 divisions, and about three or four hundred dragoons more, that had lined the hedges on both sides of their horse; when we came within 6 score of them, we mended our pace, and fell into their left

division, routing and killing several of them.

'The dragoons on both sides, seeing us so mixed with their own men that they could not fire at us, but they might kill their own men as well as ours; took horse and away they run also'.

Of an engagement on 5 June at Tog-hill during the battle of Lansdown, Atkyns reports: 'About 3 of the clock they (seeing their advantage) sent down a strong party of horse, commanded by Colonel Burrell, Major Vantruske and others; not less than 300, and five or six hundred dragoons on both sides of the hedges, to make way for their advance, and to make good their retreat.... Our horse being placed before our foot and cannon, we commanded off troop by troop; and being within half musket shot of the hedges lined on both sides by their dragoons; several horses were killed, and some of our men; their muskets playing very hard

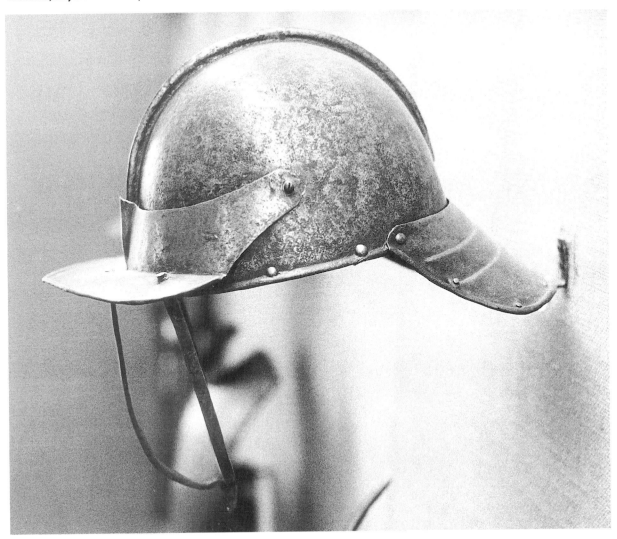

This complete set of armour represents the ideal which cavalrymen desired, but few achieved. Such armour gradually died out, due not only to cost, but also to the lighter weight and greater manoeuvrability offered by the buff coat. (By courtesy of the Board of Trustees, Royal Armouries)

upon our horse, made us retreat so disorderly, that they fell foul upon our foot, and indeed there was not room enough for us to retreat in order unless we had gone upon the very mouths of their muskets; I suppose the stratagem was to draw on their party of horse upon our foot and cannon, the better to rout them and then our horse to fall in upon them to do execution; for the dragoons making their way by pioneers, were not discovered till they shot'.

In both actions dragoons supported cavalry, providing a 'forlorn hope' or flanking fire to break up an enemy attack. Where possible, as with Okey's Dragoons at Naseby, they occupied hedges and enclosures where they would have some protection from enemy horse and foot. Despite the qualms of the theorists, the dragoon proved to be the most useful of Civil War soldiers.

Artillery

In his book *The Gunner* published in 1628 (reprinted 1643), Robert Norton divided artillery into four classes: 'Cannons of Battery, Culverins and their 'consorts', Periors shooting stone, and Mortars, murtherers, petards etc.' However, these classifications were based not on use or size of shot but rather on the proportion between total length and bore. Thus a full cannon firing a shot of 63 lb and a minion firing a shot of $3\frac{1}{4}$ lb came into the same class. In practice the distinction was between guns which fired shot heavy enough to be of use in sieges, those which were light enough to

be employed on the battlefield, and those which were used for the close defence of fortresses.

England had few modern fortresses in 1642, but many of its towns retained their medieval walls which, when reinforced by earth ramparts, could withstand a long siege conducted by an enemy without siege guns. The poor quality of the roads meant that for long journeys the heavier siege guns could only be moved by water. Many besieged garrisons owed their survival more to their inaccessibility rather than to the strength of their defences.

The Royalists were successful in their efforts to obtain a large train of artillery, and at Naseby maintained two demi-cannon (27 to 30 lb shot), two demi-culverin (9 to 10 lb shot), eight sakers (5 to 6 lb shot) and two mortars. The crew required for these guns were:

Demi-cannon:	3 gunners,	6 matrosses,	17 horses
Demi-culverin:	2 gunners,	4 matrosses,	10 horses
Saker:	2 gunners,	4 matrosses,	5 horses
Mortar:	2 gunners,	6 matrosses,	20 horses

These crews may have been armed like those of the train at the siege of Lichfield in 1643, where five gunners and 12 matrosses carried long poleaxes, and two wheelwrights carried swords.

The Royalists may have had other guns, much

The bridle gauntlet was so called because it was worn to protect the hand that held the horse bridle. A common ploy during cavalry mêlées was to try to cut an opponent's reins or slash his left arm so that he would lose control of his mount. Unlike many damaged gauntlets, this example retains the flexible hand and finger sections which permitted the small wrist movements used to control the horse. (National Army Museum)

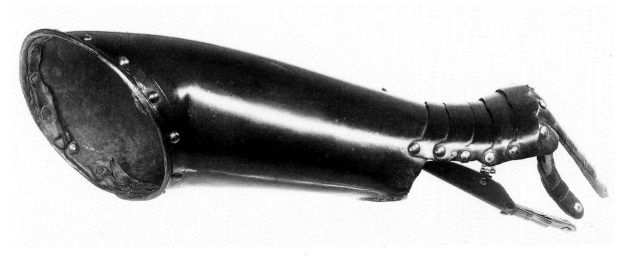

In place of a bridle gauntlet to defend his lower right arm, the cavalryman could use a padded leather arm protector. The top would fit into the cuff of a glove and the arm would be protected back to the elbow. (National Army Museum)

smaller and more mobile, attached to regiments or brigades of foot rather than to the Train of Ordnance. Many experiments had been made during European wars to construct guns which were light but which could still deliver a worthwhile charge of musket balls or roundshot. One answer was to mount several small guns together to make what were known as 'frames' or 'cases'. The most famous light artillery piece was the leather gun developed by the Swedes. This was constructed of bronze or brass tubes, about one-third of an inch thick at the muzzle, which were bound with cord an inch and a quarter thick. This was treated with plaster of Paris, and the whole covered in shrunken-on leather. Guns of this kind had to be used with care and were considered as 'one shot' weapons to be used to support an assault or as a last ditch defence. Light guns of this type were used during the Civil War and lived up to the expectations of their mobility. Two such guns accompanied the all-cavalry force which the Royalists sent to relieve Devizes, and which was victorious at Roundway Down.

Loading and firing a gun was dangerous, but not as time-consuming as some historians have claimed. Benjamin Robin's *New Principles of Gunnery*, although published a century after the start of the Civil War, explains the procedure that a Civil War artillery crew would have followed:

'Have in readiness powder, Bullets, Linstocks, Scowrers, Rammers, and the rest of your things. Stick up your Linstock to Leeward of you; then to work with your Piece. First, cleer your Piece within with the scowrer, and see that the touch hole be clear, and not stopped, and so clear, that no dirt or filth be in the same; Then let him that is by to assist, (for a Piece cannot be managed by less than two) bring the Budg-barrel with the powder just before the mouth of your Piece, put then your Ladle into the same and fill it, and if it be over-full, give it a little jog, that the overplus may fall down again into the barrel; after this, put it gently in at the mouth of the piece; even until the end of the Ladle be thrust up to the Britch end of the Piece; then must you turn the Ladle gently and softly and let it lie within the Chamber of the Piece, drawing out your Ladle almost to the Muzzle of the Piece, put it back again to take up the loose corns, which were spilt by the way, and to bring them up to the Charge of Powder; this done, the Gunner must draw out his Ladle, and take out of the Budg-barrel a second Ladle full, and so putting it in the Piece up to the former Ladle-full, then you may draw it out, and do as you did before, that no loose corns may lie in the bottom of the Piece; and in drawing out his Ladle, he must have a care that he let not fall any powder upon the ground; for it is a thing uncomly in a Gunner, to trample powder under feet. Then take a wisp of Straw, Hay or any other thing, and put it hard in at the mouth of the Piece, then turn your Ladle end for end to come to the Rammer, thrust it into the Piece after the wisp, and drive it up with it, and it will carry all the loose corns which possibly may be scattered in the Mold of the Piece; having driven the wad up to the powder, give it two or three gentle shoves to make it lie close only, but drive it not too hard least you break your powder too much, which would hinder its force; The wisp or wad being close to the powder, draw out the Rammer and put in the Bullet, which rowle gently in the Piece up to the wad that was before put in to keep up the powder; the Shot being in, put in a second wad after the Bullet, and thrust it also home to the Bullet.

Always remembering whilst the powder is putting in and wadding up, one be ready at the touch hole and keep it stopt with his thumb that no powder fly out at the touch hole, but that it be likewise filled with powder which may be supplyed out of his powder-horn'.

Artillery also fired 'murthering shot' or case-shot, which was several musket balls or pieces of scrap metal loaded in canisters of tin or lanthorn or bags of canvas. This was particularly effective when used to defend a breach or passageway, and many obsolete guns were retained in fortresses so that they could give one devastating shot at any attackers approaching them.

Civil War artillery has a reputation for inaccuracy, and a slow rate of fire; but this was not the view of those who faced it, as borne out by soldiers like Elias Archer. The Royalist garrison at Basing House was equipped with three gunners, two 6 lb and one 3 lb guns; for these they had 25 roundshot and five case-shot per gun. Archer reports that men from Sir William Waller's own company of his regiment of foot fell foul of these guns during an attack:

'Sir William's Captaine Lieutenant by an unfortunate mistake in the way to the place where he was designed to goe on, went with his party which he then commanded up a lane where the enemy had planted two drakes with case-shot, which being fired slew both him and many of his men, whose losse was very much lamented'.

Further Reading
Contemporary sources:
Richard Atkyns, *The Vindication of Richard Atkyns* (in *Military Memoirs: the Civil War*, ed. Peter Young, London 1967)
Nathaneal Burt, *Militarie Instructions*, or *The Souldier tried for the use of the Dragoon*, Wapping 1644. (In John Adair, *By the Sword Divided*, London 1983)
John Cruso, *Militarie Instructions for the Cavallerie*, Cambridge 1632
J.B., *Some Brief Instructions for the Exercising of the Horse-Troopes* (in William Barriffe, *Militarie Discipline*, London, 1661)

Gervase Markham *The Souldiers Accidence*, London 1625
Gervase Markham *The Souldiers Grammar*, London 1627
Gervase Markham *The Souldiers Exercise*, London 1643
George Monk, *Observations upon Military and Political Affairs*, London 1671
Robert Norton, *The Gunner: Shewing the Whole Practice of Artillerie*, London 1628
Benjamin Robins, *New Principles of Gunnery*, London 1742
Sir John Smythe, *Instructions, Observations and Orders Mylitarie*, London 1595

The arms of a harquebusier in 1643. From the Littlecote collection, this set typifies the classic idea of the Cromwellian cavalry trooper, yet it may date from a time when Cromwell was a little-known captain of horse. (By courtesy of the Board of Trustees, Royal Armouries)

Sir James Turner, *Pallas Armata: Militarie Essayes of the Ancient Grecian, Roman and Modern Art of War*, 1670-1

John Vernon, *The young Horse-Man or the Honest Plain-Dealing Cavalier*, London 1644

Robert Ward, *Animadversions of Warre*, London 1639

Secondary sources:

L. Boynton, *The Elizabethan Militia 1558-1638*, London 1967

C.H. Firth, *Cromwell's Army*, London 1902

P. Haythornthwaite, *The English Civil War 1642–51: An Illustrated Military History*, Poole 1983

P. Young, *Edgehill 1642: The Campaign and the Battle*, Kineton 1967

P. Young, *The English Civil War Armies*, Reading 1973 (Osprey Men-at-Arms 14)

English Civil War Notes and Queries—the only magazine dedicated to the period. Partizan Press, 26 Cliffsea Grove, Leigh-on-Sea, SS9 1NQ.

Thousands of people regularly re-enact battles of the English Civil War. If you would like information about this exciting hobby, write to the above address.

Trained Band Cavalry

"The Trayned Bands of the severall Counties of England and Wales Collected Feb 9th 1637" [From SP 16/381/66. The last full muster of the trained bands before the Civil Wars shows that some counties still raised the types of horse that had been specified in Tudor times. The large numbers of horse raised in the counties that were to form the Eastern Association give some indication of the resources that were available for the formation of Cromwell's formidable cavalry force.]

COUNTIES	FOOTE			HORSE	
Anglesey	259	Musketts		25	
	141	Corsletts	= 400		
Bedford	296	m		40 Lancers	
	204	c	= 500	30 Light	= 70
Berks	680	m		59 Curass.	
	420	c	= 1100	31 Harq.	= 90
				30	
Brecknock	180	m			
	120	c	= 300		
Bristol	210	m			
	90	c	= 300		
Bucks	400	m		47 Lancers	
	200	c	= 600	55 Light	= 102
Cambridge	540	m		30 Carb.	
	460	c	= 1000	50 Drag.	= 80
Cardigan	150	m		35	
	150	c	= 300		
Carmarthen	220	m		35	
	330	c	= 550		
Carnarvon	100	m		25	
	100	c	= 200		
Chester	359	m			
	240	c	= 600		
Cinque Ports	1649	m		14	
	326	c	= 1975		
Cornwall	3850	m		14	
	2310	c	= 6160		
Cumberland					
Darby	239	m		33 Curass.	
	161	c	= 400	41 Drag.	= 74
Denbeigh	300	m		50	
	200	c	= 500		
Devon	4253	m		126	
	2509	c	= 6762		
Dorsett	1444	m		100	
	696	c	= 2140		
Durham	532	m		60	
	500	c	= 1032		
Essex	2152	m		200 Light	
	1878	c	= 4030	50 Lancers	= 250
Flinte	140	m		30	
	60	c	= 200		
Glamorgan	200	m		36	
	200	c	= 400		
Gloucester	1826	m		200	
	1294	c	= 3120		
Hartford	750	m		27 Lancers	
	750	c	= 1500	53 Light	= 80
Hereford	280	m		90	
	200	c	= 480		
Huntingdon	240	m		20 Lancers	
	160	c	= 400	30 Light	= 50
Kent	2910	m		293	
	1757	c	= 4667		
Lancaster	420	m		25 Lancers	
	180	c	= 600	81 Light	= 106
Leicester	290	m		38 Lancers	
	210	c	= 500	62 Light	= 100
Lincolne	1080	m		230	
	720	c	= 1800		

The Plates

A: The Cuirassier

The cuirassier of the Civil War did not wear a full suit of armour. Thick leather riding boots were worn in place of armour for the legs and feet, and only the front of the thighs were protected by cuisses.

The closed helm (1) and (2) came in many forms, with varying degrees of protection for the face weighed against the angle of vision and amount of oxygen provided to the wearer. Some cuirassiers may have opted to wear open helmets, but Sir Arthur Haslerigge wore a 'headpiece musket proof' of sufficient thickness to withstand Richard Atkyns' pistol shot.

The gorget (3) had tapes with which to attach the shoulder pieces (9). The back (6) and breastplate (4) strapped together so that they could be used independently of the rest of the armour. The placcate (5), a thick reinforcing plate which fitted on to the front of the breastplate, and the guard de reine (7), providing protection to the lower back, were often discarded during the Civil War as the extra protection they offered was not con-

COUNTIES	FOOTE		HORSE			COUNTIES	FOOTE		HORSE		
London	3000 m					Salop	341 m		100		
	3000 c	= 6000					259 c	= 600			
Merioneth	100 m		15			Somerset	2403 m		218 Harq.		
	100 c	= 200					1597 c	= 4000	82 Curass.	= 300	
Middlesex	928 m		80			Southampton	2854 m		170		
	653 c	= 1581					1945 c	= 4799			
Monmouth	200 m		47			Stafford	248 m		30 Light		
	200 c	= 400					152 c	= 400	73 Curass.	= 103	
Montgomery	150 m		50			Suffolke	2359 m		300 Curass.		
	150 c	= 300					1789 c	= 4148			
Norfolk	2910 m		320 Harq.			Surrey	604 m		66 Harq.		
	2407 c	= 5317	80 Curass.	= 400			896 c	= 1500	63 Curass	= 129	
Northampton	284 m		58 Cur.			Sussex	1804 m		160		
	295 c	= 579	50 Light	= 108			1000 c	= 2804			
Northumberland						Warwick	357 m		88 Curass.		
							243 c	= 600			
Nottingham	282 m		50 Curass.			Westmerland					
	125 c	= 407	10 Drag.	= 60							
Oxon	500 m		40 Lancers			Worcester	491 m		70		
	350 c	= 850	40 Light	= 80			309 c	= 800			
Pembroke	276 m		57			Wiltes	1285m		30 Lancers		
	281 c	= 557					1115c	= 2400	126 Light	= 156	
Radnor	112 m		25			Yorke	6720 m		365 Curass.		
	88 c	= 200					5521 c	= 12241	35 Drag.	= 400	
Rutland	60 m		30 Light			**Total**	**54,517 m**				
	40 c	= 100					**39,081 c**	**= 93,718**	**5,239**		

'Na. That by letters from the Board of the 10th of July 1626 to the Lo. Clifford Lord Lieut of the Counties of Cumberland, Northumberland and Westmerland. It was directed, that there should be forthwith raised and Trained 500 Foote and 100 Horse within the Countie of Northumberland, and 400 Foote more in the Towne of Newcastle, and within the Counties of Cumberland and Westmerland jointly 500 Foote and 100 Horse; All the said Foote to be halfe Pikes, halfe Musketts, And all the said Horse to be Hargobusiers. But no account hath beene had herto quick concerning the same.

Na. also that in the Muster Roll returned for the County of Leicester, there is besides the 500 Trayned men aforemencioned, 500 Private Armes, whereof 299 m and 201 Cors.

Memorial that by the letters from the Board of the 10th July 1626 there is directed to be kept in Magazine in the several Counties of England and Wales in all 247 Last, a quarter and half of Powder'.

Commissions for Raising Royalist Cavalry

'A Briefe of such Comissions for the raising of horse and dragoons, as have passed under The Great Seale and sign manuall since the 10th of October last 1642.' [British Museum Add. Mss 18980 f20.] King Charles granted commissions freely, but many of the regiments and troops listed below never materialized. The huge bodies of up to 2,000 dragoons were intended to hold and exploit the counties to which they were appointed, but these great plans came to nothing.]

Lord Andover	500 horse.	11 October
Sir John Berkeley	500 horse in Cornwall	
Richard Herbert	1 troop	16 August
Sir Thomas Salusbury	200 Dragoons in Denbigh	1 November
Earl of Chesterfield	Regt. 500 Dragoons in Derbyshire	24 November
Alan Butler	Regt. 2000 Dragoons	13 November
James Young	1 troop (P. Maurice)	13 November
Edward Stamford	1 troop (Lo. Digby)	20 August
Gerard Croker	1 troop	17 September
David Walker	1 troop (Lo. Digby)	6 September
Sir Robert Howard	1 Regt. horse	25 September
Sir James Hamilton	1 Regt. horse	
Earl of Crawford	1 Regt. horse	25 September
Sir Faithful Fortescue	1 Regt. horse	25 September
Earl of Northampton	1 Regt. 500	25 September
Robert Key	S. M. to Col Croker	
George Heron	1 Regt. 500 in Northumberland	26 November
Lo. Chandos	1 Regt.	29 November
James Young	to be Col. of Regt.	8 December
Lo. Capell	1 Regt.	24 November
John Heynes	1 troop of Dragoons.	8 December
Samuell Sandys	1 Regt. Worcestershire	
Sir Vincent Corbett	2000 Dragoons in Shropshire	10 December
Thomas Hammer	2000 Dragoons in Flynt & Denbyshire.	
Thomas Cumberland	1 Regt. Staffordshire	
Lo. Chandos	500 Dragoons	17 December
Lo. Grey	1 Regt. Northumberland	19 December
John Cherto	1 Regt.	22 December
John Fitzherbert	1 Regt. Horse or Drag. in Derbyshire	25 December
Capt. Thomas Howard	1 Regt.	31 December
Charles Cavendish	1 Regt.	31 December
Sir Richard Byron	1 troop + 1 troop Dragoons	20 December
Lewis Kirk	600 Dragoons	
Arther Hopton	1 troop under Col. Gerard Crocker	31 December
Capt. Richard Hastings	1 troop under Thomas Howard	31 December
Alan Apsley	1 troop Dragoons	24 December
Sir Vincent Corbet	1 troop Dragoons Salop	
Sir William Pennyman	1 Regt. horse Darby + 5 officers	
Col. Charles Gerard	1 Regt.	
Sir Thomas Aston	500 Dragoons Cheshire	
Sir Ralph Dutton	1 Regt. horse	
Earl of Crawford	1 Regt. horse + 1 Regt dragoons in Cumberland	
Richard Atkins	1 troop	22 January
Henry Berry	500 horse	2 February
Sir Richard Willys	1 Regt. 600 horse	29 January
Sir Baynham Throckmtn.	2000 Dragoons	
Wally Leigh	1 troop (P. Maurice)	
Edmund Chamberlayne	1 Regt. 500 Dragoons Oxon	7 February
Lo. Dunsmore	500 horse Warwickshire	

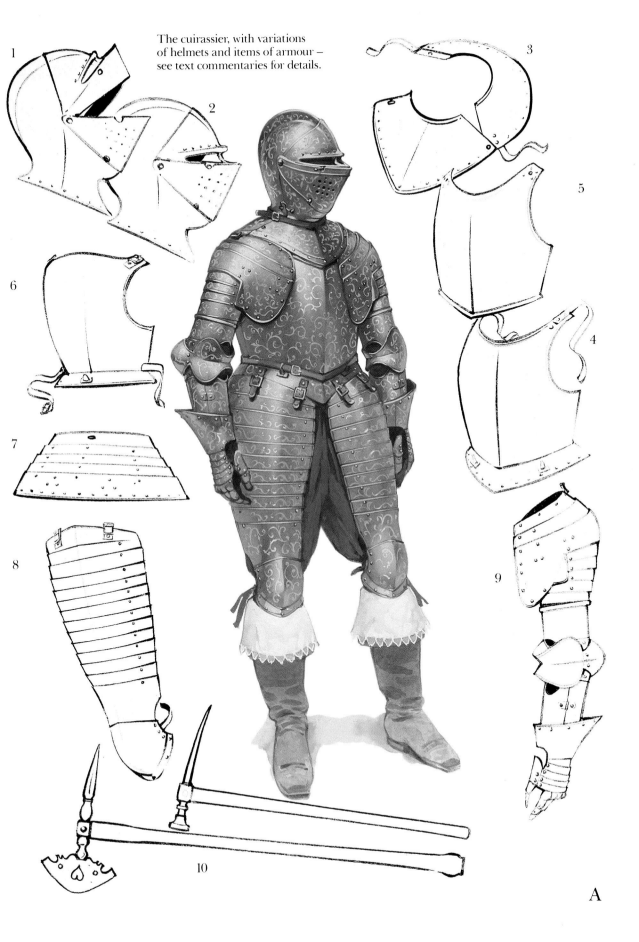

The cuirassier, with variations
of helmets and items of armour –
see text commentaries for details.

1

2

3

5

6

4

7

8

9

10

A

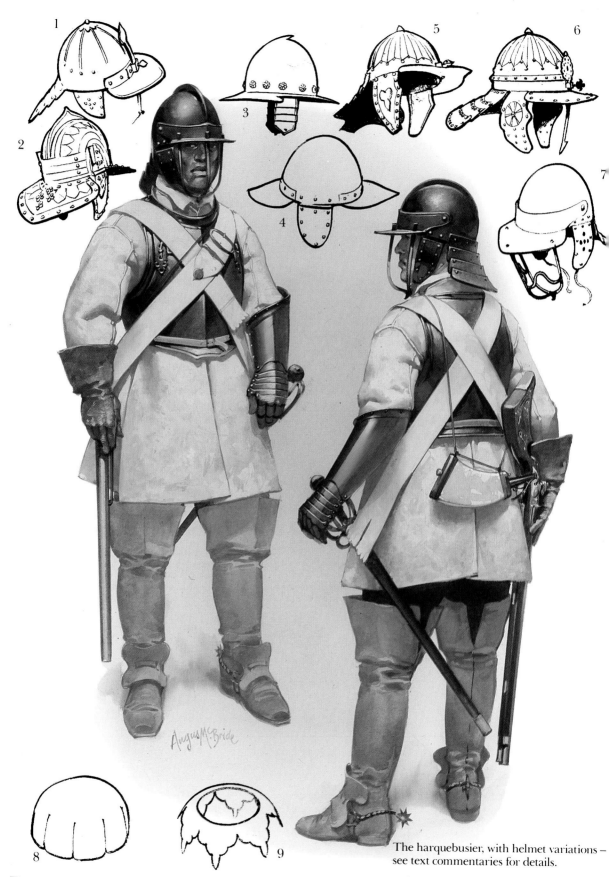

1

2

3

4

5

6

7

8

9

The harquebusier, with helmet variations –
see text commentaries for details.

B

Royalist Horse, 1642:
1: French influence
2: Dutch influence
3: Improvisation

C

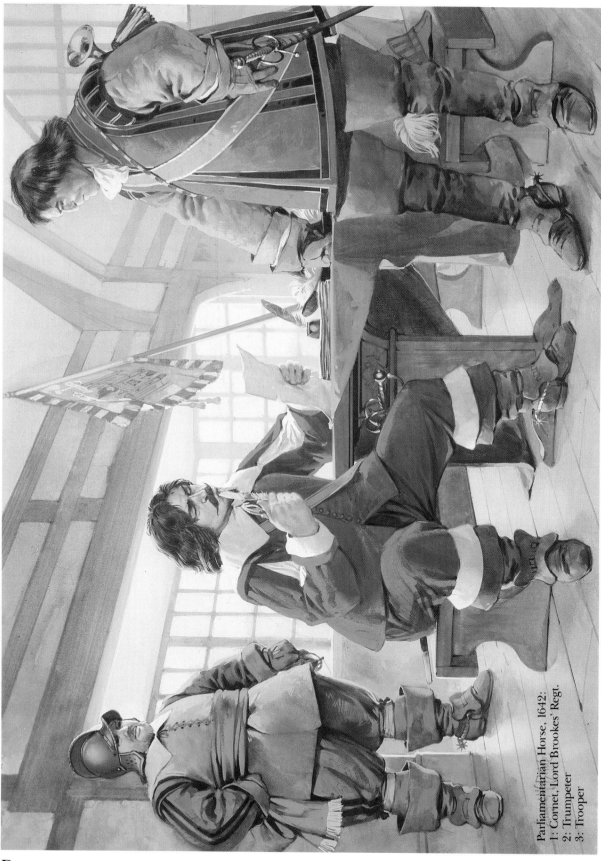

Parliamentarian Horse, 1642:
1: Cornet, Lord Brookes' Regt.
2: Trumpeter
3: Trooper

D

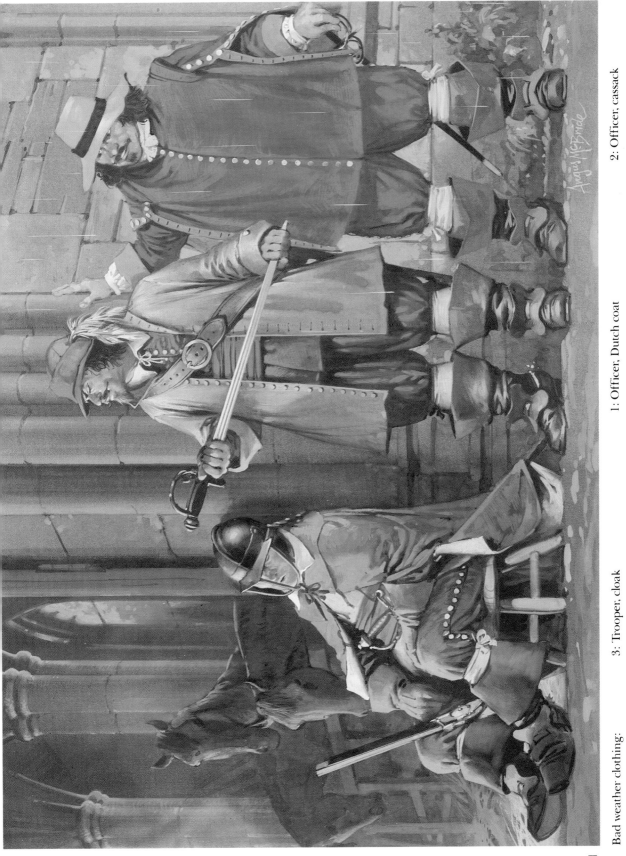

Bad weather clothing: 3: Trooper, cloak   1: Officer, Dutch coat   2: Officer, cassack

E

'Haslerigge's Lobsters' at Roundway Down – see text commentaries for details.

Angus McBride

ONLY iN HEAVEN!

F

New Model Horse, 1645:
1: Royalist cornet
2: Officer, New Model Army
3: Trooper, New Model Army

G

New Model Dragoons, 1645:
1: Officer, Okey's Regt.
2: Mounted dragoon, Okey's Regt.
3: Dragoon, Okey's Regt.

2

3

1

H

2   3

Royalists, 1645:
1: Cavalry trooper
2: Officer
3: Dragoon

I   1

Siege lines:
1: Engineer
2: Dismounted cavalryman
3: Sniper

Angus McBride

2

1

J

Artilleryman, with tools – see
text commentaries for details.

1

2

3

4

9

8

10

11

6

5

7

12

K

sidered worth their weight.

The articulated cuisses (8) were difficult to make and were often the first part of the cuirassier's armour to be discarded. One surviving cuisse has been made of leather to replicate the metal cuisse belonging to the other leg.

The pouldrons (9) to defend the shoulders and vambraces to protect the arms also disappeared in favour of thick buff sleeves as manoeuvrability and cost become more important than protection. Metal bridle gauntlets which covered the bridle hand and arm to the elbow were introduced, but leather gloves replaced the fully armoured gauntlets.

The spiked axe or hammer (10) was a weapon specifically designed to defeat the armour of the cuirassier. Although it was not universally carried there are several references to its use and effectiveness.

B: The Harquebusier

The quality and quantity of the harquebusier's equipment preserved at Littlecote House can be regarded as a model for any period of the war. Armed with two flintlock pistols and a flintlock carbine, Popham's troopers were protected by tri-bar helmets, back and breastplates, long buff coats and metal bridle gauntlets. Baldrics, carbine belts and some powder flasks have also survived along with the armour and buff coat of Popham himself.

The majority of the helmets used by cavalry during the Civil War conformed to a basic design of a skull with peak, a rear peak or tail to protect the neck, and flaps to defend the ears. The 'lobster tail' helmet (1) with a single bar protecting the face was common in Europe. This example has re-inforcing bars built into the crown, and a loop at the top so that it can be carried strung from the saddle.

The type of helmet shown as (2) is less common, perhaps because it would have been more expensive. The crown has been made in two halves and joined along the rim, with large front and rear peaks riveted on. Unlike the other helmets shown here this was probably the property of an officer.

The next helmet (3) shows some characteristics of the cabasset morion popular for infantrymen around 1600; it may be that this is an old helmet

The buff coat of a Royalist officer. The edge of the upper sleeve clearly shows the thickness of the leather used for the main part of the coat. The lower part of the sleeve is made of thinner leather to enable the wearer to move his arms freely. The seams are butt-jointed rather than overlapped, except for the standing collar, which is inset. (National Army Museum)

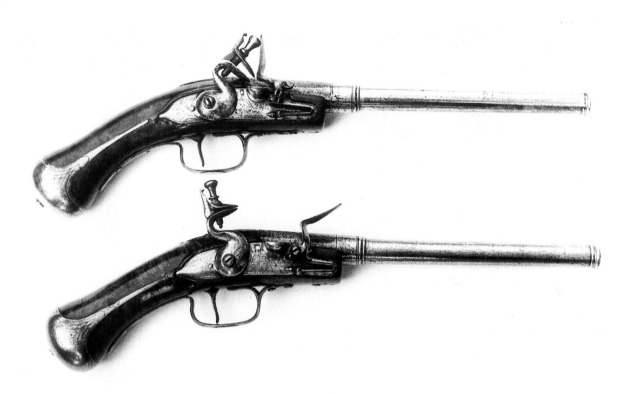

Although these rifled pistols are thought to date from 1660 they are of a type used in the Civil Wars. The barrel is made in two parts and unscrews to allow powder and ball to be loaded. With the barrel replaced the pistol is fired and the ball expands into the grooves in the barrel.(National Army Museum)

that was adapted for cavalry use by the addition of peaks at front and back. Very similar in style, if not in quality, is the home-made helmet (4), perhaps made by a village blacksmith. Despite its poor appearance it is functional and robust.

Helmets (5) and (6) were imported from the Continent and were made with very strong—but difficult to manufacture—fluted crowns. A few examples of this type may have found their way into England with soldiers returning from the European wars. The tri-bar pot (7) was the most popular helmet of the Civil Wars, but this example is uncommon in having curved reinforcing bars added.

Items (8) and (9) are not helmets proper but 'secrets' worn sewn into the crown of a felt hat or Montero cap to provide the wearer with basic protection.

C: Royalist Horse, 1642

This Royalist family preparing to join the king's army on the field of Edgehill show the wide range of experience and equipment seen in the early armies.

C1: The French influence

This costume is based upon a *c.* 1638 set of clothing and equipment surviving in the *Musée de l'Armée* in Paris. The eldest son of the family has returned from service in the French Wars in response to the news of troubles in England. His metal 'hat' is not unique for both King Charles and John Bradshaw (President of the Court at the king's trial) had similar protective headwear. The long-barrelled pistol he is examining is also a memento from his French service; the wheellock was more commonly used on the Continent, and French pistols were noted for having barrels so long that they would not fit into English holsters.

C2: The Dutch influence

The head of the household looks back to his military service with the Dutch army in the early part of the Thirty Years' War. His armour, like the ruff he wears, is some years behind the current fashions, yet in an army starved of equipment it may secure him a place in the King's Lifeguard of Horse—if his income can support the lifestyle of the 'troop of shew'. His helmet is of the burgonet

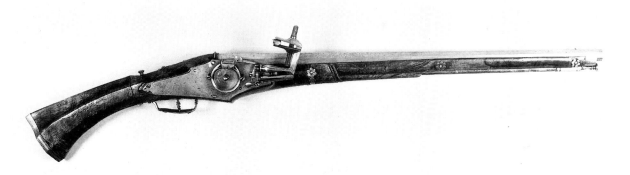

The wheellock was fired by a spark produced by pyrites held against a revolving serrated wheel. The wheel was driven by a v-spring wound by a key which fitted onto a nut at the centre of the wheel. (National Army Museum)

type which replaced closed helmets in the late 16th century. This process continued, and by the time of the Civil War open-faced helmets based on the eastern European 'Zishagge' were in fashion.

C3: Improvisation

With no time to purchase new arms, and with any remaining military equipment being desperately hunted out from the homes of local Parliamentarians, the Royalist gentry did their best to equip their retainers. A medieval sallet helmet with a Civil War-style metal peak survives in the Tower of London, and this groom is doing his best to provide himself with such a helmet. He has no pistols or armour and will fall into the back ranks

armed only with his sword. He will need to provide himself with a pair of strong riding boots to protect his legs and knees from being crushed by his comrades' horses in a charge.

D: Parliamentarian Horse, 1642

Possession of the major national armouries should have given Parliament all the arms it needed, but the wars against the Scots and the Irish Rebellion had greatly reduced these stores. Like the Royalists the Parliamentarians imported several thousand weapons in time for Edgehill, and other weapons were provided by donation or by recruits bringing their own equipment.

The ordinary cavalryman would have carried pistols of simple manufacture. The early flintlock mechanism was unreliable, and additional safety features (such as the 'dog catch' seen on the top pistol) were necessary when the weapon was to be carried ready to fire in the holster of a charging horse. (National Army Museum)

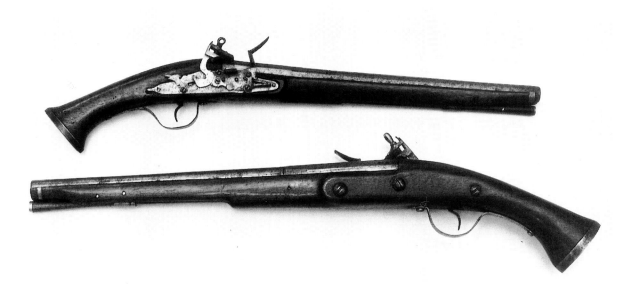

D1: Cornet of Horse

Officers of all ranks provided their own clothing and equipment and this cornet of Lieutenant-Colonel Sir Edward Peto's troop of Lord Brookes' regiment wears a plain civilian suit. The main body of his doublet is made from four pieces of cloth, giving back and side vents as well as a front opening to be closed with closely spaced cloth buttons. The effect is to form a four-tabbed doublet with the front tabs set on a curve to accentuate the 'belly', a final reminder of the 'peascod' padding of Tudor times. His breeches are tied around the waist, and extend some way below the knee to be met by the boot hose which protect finer stockings from being rubbed by the boots.

D2: Trumpeter

Trumpeters wore different and more colourful clothing than the troopers of their regiments. In 1647 Colonel Thorpe spent £21 13s. 4d. on 'Clothes and other necessaries of the Trumpets'. This figure is taken from a trumpeter who appears in several versions of a contemporary Dutch painting. He wears a cassock with hanging sleeves over a buff coat; and has a Montero cap, a style of headgear worn by all ranks during the Civil War. As in the Dutch picture this trumpeter is acting as a messenger, a rôle often give to musicians.

D3: Parliamentarian Trooper

In 1642 Parliament aimed to raise 4,500 cavalry, but few sets of armour for horsemen were available from the arsenals at the Tower of London and Hull. This soldier is equipped with an old burgonet helmet taken from a Royalist supporter, which has been painted with lampblack to protect it from rust. Like the men of Sir Thomas Sandy's Troop he has been given 10s. to buy a sash (often called a scarf in contemporary documents) to identify his loyalty to Parliament. He has been lucky that his troop's captain has purchased some sleeveless buff coats, one of which he wears over his civilian clothing.

E: Bad weather clothing

Taking advantage of their greater mobility, cavalrymen could often beat their infantry comrades to the best billets. A cavalry regiment might have to

John Okey, Colonel of the New Model Regiment of Dragoons, recorded an unusual charge by his men at the battle of Naseby: 'I ... caused all my men to mount and to charge into their foot, which accordingly they did; and took all their Colours, and 500 Prisoners, besides what we killed, and all their Armes. After this the King his Horse drew up into a body againe: and then I drew up my Dragoons, and, charged the King's Regiment of Horse, and they faced about and run away'. (D. Carter collection)

be split up between half a dozen small villages to find shelter and sustenance. The church was the largest building and was often pressed into service.

E1: The Dutch coat

This officer is wearing a 'Dutch coat', which became a popular form of overcoat during the war and was often worn over armour in battle. Richard Atkyns reported that at Little Dean on 11 April 1643, 'the enemy were upon me, cutting my coat upon my armour in several places'. The Montero cap was worn by several high-ranking officers, one report mentioning Sir Thomas Fairfax as wearing a red Montero like that worn by a Royalist commander, probably Prince Rupert.

E2: The cassock

The cassock worn by this officer is a more expensive garment than the Dutch coat. The side seams and the seams of the sleeves are made to unbutton. By buttoning an edge of the sleeve to each side of the main body the garment can be transformed into a cloak. This flexibility requires a great number of buttons. The Earl of Essex maintained a 30-strong personal guard of halberdiers each of whose grey cassocks had 180 silver and orange buttons.

E3: The cloak

The trooper wears a cheap but practical cloak, and there is evidence that cloaks of various lengths were worn by cavalry in place of the coats worn by infantry. A troop of horse are shown in cloaks on the monument of Edward St John at Lydiard Tregoze church. Sir Thomas Dallison recorded that he had 300 or 400 yards of red cloth to make cloaks for Prince Rupert's regiment. The cavalry of the New Model Army were equipped with

S.ʳ William Balfore etc:-

Sir William Balfore was one of many Scottish professional soldiers who fought in the English armies during the Civil War. Balfore began the war serving under the Earl of Essex, but took his brigade to support Waller for the Cheriton campaign in 1644. Balfore considered himself Waller's equal in rank, but history has awarded the victory to Waller. (D. Carter collection)

cloaks for their campaigns in Ireland, the broadcloth being shipped out and made up locally. In 1650, 15,000 yards of broadcloth at 11s. 3d. per yard was supplied for horsemen's cloaks, and 1,178 yards of Spanish cloth at £3 17s. for officers' cloaks.

F: The destruction of Haslerigge's 'Lobsters'

The battle of Roundway Down near Devizes saw a confrontation between two doctrines of cavalry tactics. The result was the eclipse of the heavily armoured cuirassier by the lighter harquebusier; and the triumph of the charge to contact by a three-deep formation over horsemen relying on firepower and drawn up six deep. Richard Atkyns described the battle:

The right Hon:.ᵇᶜ Edward Earle of Manchester &c: major Generall of the Association

The Earl of Manchester is best remembered for his long-running battle with Cromwell over the recruitment of religious Independents into the Eastern Association. Manchester was one of the commanders removed by the Self-Denying Ordinance which excluded members of Parliament from military command. (D. Carter collection)

'We lost no time, but marched towards the enemy, who stood towards the top of the hill; the foot in the middle between two wings of horse, and the cannon before the foot ... then forlorn-hopes out of each army were drawn out, and the Lord Wilmott's Major, Paul Smith commanded ours, who did it with that gallantry, that he beat them into the very body of their left wing, and put them out of order; which we took advantage of, and immediately charged the whole body; the charge was so sudden that I had hardly time to put on my arms, we advanced a full trot 3 deep, and kept in order; the enemy kept their station, and their right wing of horse being cuirassiers, were I'm sure five, if not six deep, in so close order, that Punchinello himself had he been there, could not have gotten in to them.

All the horse on the left hand of Prince Maurice his regiment, had none to charge; we charging the very utmost man of their right wing ... for though they were above twice our numbers; they being six deep, in close order and we but three deep, and open (by reason of our sudden charge) we were without them at both ends: the cannoneers seeing our resolution, did not fire their cannon. No men ever charged better than ours did that day'.

Haslerigge's regiment was routed and driven over the cliffs which surround the Down. The flag shown is that of Haslerigge's own troop; the other cornets of his regiment depicted an arm holding a sword emerging from a cloud against a green background.

G: The New Model Horse, 1645

In 1645 Parliament sent its newly formed New Model Army into the field in an effort to break the deadlock of the previous year. The replacement of unsuccessful commanders and the provision of £80,000 to equip and supply the new force was intended to produce an army which would have the determination and stamina to finish the war.

G1: Royalist Cornet

The buff coat worn by this Royalist cornet is

Three cavalry carbines from the Littlecote collection. All are pictured at the 'half cock' position used when loading and when the gun was being carried while loaded. In each case the dog catch is engaged in case the internal spring fails, firing the weapon. (By courtesy of the Board of Trustees, Royal Armouries)

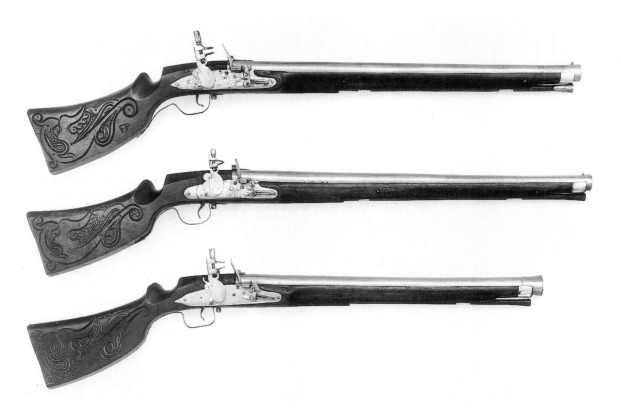

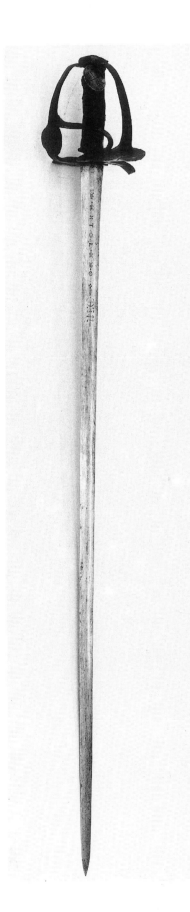

based upon a fine example now housed at the Museum of London. The Civil War cavalryman wearing hooped sleeves has become a cliché of Victorian illustrations, but this buff coat features close-set narrow metal braid stitched in hoops on to the buff sleeves. The cut of the coat, its high standing collar and the metal clasps identify it as an officer's garment.

G2: New Model Officer of Horse

The defensive equipment of this officer of the New Model Army is based upon surviving items now at the Royal Armouries. The buff coat has an unusual wrapover skirt which is held in place by a cord, and demonstrates that the skirts of a buff coat were not intended to divide around the saddle boss when the wearer was mounted. Such a coat would have covered not only the upper legs of the rider but the saddle as well. As a senior officer he has a large gorget rather than back and breastplates, valuing agility over protection. His helmet is a fine example of a musket-proof Zishagge, and is of much higher quality than those issued to his soldiers.

G3: New Model Trooper

The surviving accounts of the first months of the New Model Army's existence give many details of items of equipment issued to cavalrymen. Suits of 'armes' consisting of tri-bar pot helmets and back and breastplates are recorded, along with pairs of pistols in calfskin holsters and carbines suspended on shoulder belts. What is missing from these accounts is any reference to riding boots, gloves or gauntlets, buff coats or any uniform. C.H. Firth in *Cromwell's Army* advanced the theory that the troopers wore sleeved buff coats, as the agitators for the cavalry in the army debates after the war are always referred to as 'buff coats'. If this was the case it may be that the buff coats were purchased by the soldiers themselves, or by their troop commanders, along with other items of clothing. What is clear from the New Model accounts of 1645 is that a great deal of equipment was still being purchased when the army had

A simple sword of the type used by cavalrymen during the Civil War. The fencing rapier was used in the early months of the war, but the stout-bladed slashing sword was soon found to be more useful in mounted combat. (National Army Museum)

A Bridge made of Punts.

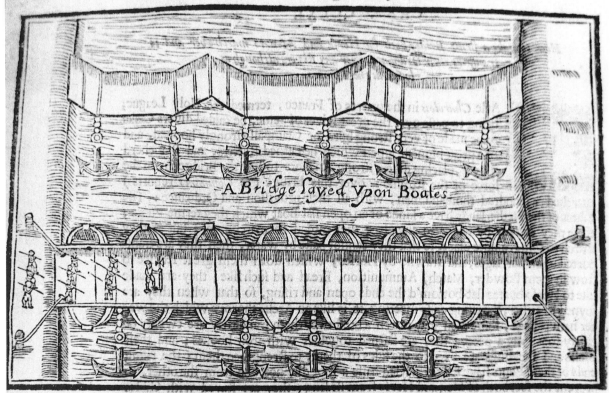

A Bridge layed Vpon Boates

The Treſſels which the King of *Sweden* made his Bridge upon to paſſe over the
Lech into *Bavaria*, the feet of the Treſſels had weights upon their Ledges to hold
them downe in the water.

taken the field for the Naseby campaign. Parliament was able to make up the New Model cavalry regiments by joining together remnants of units from Essex's, Manchester's and Waller's armies. It may be that during its first campaigns the New Model Horse wore either their old uniforms or clothes they purchased themselves.

H: New Model Dragoons

Although his rôle in battle was ill-defined by military theorists, the dragoon proved to be one of the most useful soldiers of the Civil Wars. Outpost duty and the gathering of contributions were the common tasks of the dragoon, but his ability to keep pace with cavalry on the march made him invaluable for raiding parties.

H1: Officer of Okey's Dragoons, 1645

In 1648 the dragoon Lieutenant-Colonel John Lilburne was described as wearing a 'short red coat', and this has been taken as evidence both that the New Model dragoons wore red coats like the foot, and that officers wore uniform coats like those of their men. However, it was not the custom for officers of any type to wear a uniform before the 1680s; and it is more likely that New Model dragoon officers followed the normal practice and wore individual clothing that they had purchased themselves. This officer could therefore equally well be in command of an infantry, cavalry or dragoon unit.

H2: Mounted Dragoon of Okey's Regiment, 1645

Little of the equipment listed in the accounts of the New Model Army is specified as being for issue to dragoons. Saddles for dragoons cost only 7s. 6d. and are differentiated from those for cavalry troopers which cost 16s. 6d. An example in the Royal Armouries shows why. The dragoon was not intended to charge into contact and therefore his saddle has no front and back supports to help him remain seated during impact. Both the dragoons depicted here are equipped with bando-

Robert Ward describes the Pontoon Bridges thus: 'The Netherlands have a kinde of open flat Boat which thay terme Punts; these they convey by water to any place they intend to march over; but if they march to some remote place, so that they cannot passe by water, then they are transported upon Carriages, and drawne by Horses ...foure men may march a brest over them; and they are twenty or thirty foot long a peece....'

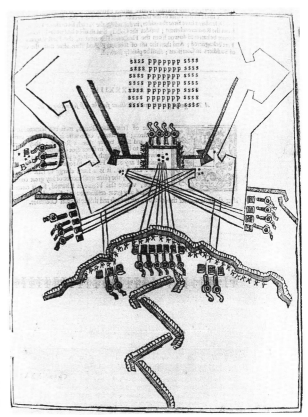

This diagram shows how to position artillery to create a breach in a fortress and to provide suppressive fire against the defenders. The shaded areas inside the fortress have been constructed to cover the breach, but the battery marked 'B' has been raised on a platform to neutralise these new defences.

liers of the type specified in the New Model Accounts for 1645 rather than with cartridge boxes. Some 2,200 'cartridges' were made, one order specifying '1,200 Cartridges the boxes of stronge plate covered with black leather 700 of them halfe round & the other 500 double at Xd a peece'. There is no evidence that these items were intended for the dragoons, and reconstructions which depict them as crude versions of the 18th century cartridge box worn around the waist are entirely speculative.

H3: Dragoon of Okey's Regiment, 1645

The Order Books do reveal something of the muskets carried by dragoons in the New Model Army. A contract of 22 December 1645 for a total of 1,000 'Dragoone Musketts' specifies that they must be 'Snaphance Musketts full bore & proofe & four foote longe at xiiii s[hillings] iiii [pence] a peece to be brought into the Tower of London 25

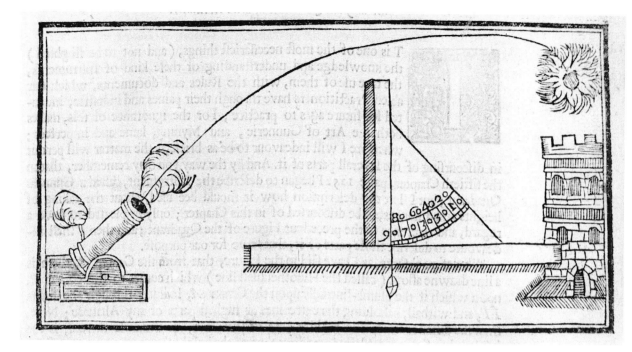

The quadrant was used to determine the angle of elevation of a mortar. 'The use of it is thus, by laying the long Rule cross the mouth of the Peece, you shall immediately perceive at what degree the said Morter Peece is elevated by the Plumb-line.'

Two trumpeters of the New Model Army, taken from Sprigge's map of the Battle of Naseby. Their trumpet banners and waist sashes are clearly shown, and they may be wearing sleeveless buff coats over doublets.

of them everie moneth'. Records of 1649 show that dragoons were issued with firearms with swivels, indicating that they were carried hanging from shoulder belts. This would have been very clumsy with a musket 4ft long, and it may be that weapons with shorter barrels were in use in 1649. There is no record of the clothing issued to dragoons and it has generally been assumed that they wore the same coats as the foot. The illustrations of New Model Army soldiers which date from the late 1640s—such as that of the trial of King Charles, and Sprigge's panorama of the battle of Naseby—show soldiers in wide-brimmed hats. However, the records of clothing issue for the first Civil War demonstrate that the issue of some form of cap was much more common. This dragoon wears the knitted Monmouth cap, which was the cheapest form of headwear, costing as little as 6d. each.

I: Royalists in 1645

As the Civil War dragged on and neither side could look forward to an early victory, the Royalist forces began to undergo a change of leadership. The local nobility and gentry who had raised their counties for the king could not be expected to ruthlessly extract resources from their neighbours at a rate sufficient to keep the Royalist armies in the field. The answer was to employ

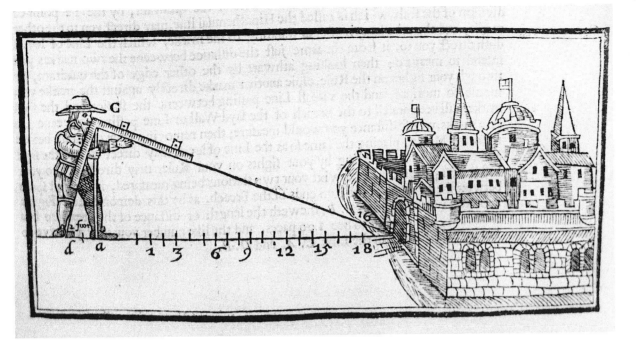

A method of measuring distance to a hostile fortress using a carpenter's square; this method was used to determine ranges and the siting of trenches.

professional soldiers in areas well away from their homes, but increased efficiency was bought at the cost of a brutalising of the war and the alienation of many of the king's supporters.

I1: Royalist Trooper with a buff girdle

The Royalists had problems equipping their forces for the battle of Edgehill, but during the winter of 1642–3 Oxford became the hub of a supply organisation which, while not rivalling the output of London, was to keep the king's soldiers equipped up to the end of the war. This soldier is well equipped with back and breast; but has opted for a buff girdle, which Monk describes as 'A Girdle of double Buff about eight inches broad, which is to be worn under the skirts of his Doublet, and to be hooked into his Doublet, and made so that it may be fastned together before. If you find Buff to be scarce and dear, you may make those Girdles of Buff before spoken of with Bull Hides or good Oxes Hides, dressed like Buff'. He wears a red sash to show his allegiance to the king, but many soldiers (like his drunken comrade) wore sashes in the personal colour of their own commander.

I2: Royalist Officer

The more wealthy officers of both armies went to war dressed in considerable luxury compared to the simple uniforms of their men. The Scottish professional James Carr, serving as a lieutenant-colonel of a Parliamentary dragoon regiment, reported that when he was captured at Cirencester on 2 February 1643 he had lost:

'One sute of Spanish Cloth layd with
    silver lace £7
A long Riding Coate of the same £2
A doublet of Buck Leather and breaches £3
A dutch Coat lyned with Foxes £4
A scarlett mantire (scull protector) layd
    with silver lace .... 30s.

I3: Royalist Dragoon

This dragoon has been hastily transformed from a musketeer by abandoning the rest belonging to his matchlock musket. Unlike the snaphance the matchlock required a piece of burning matchcord to fire it, and this must have been very difficult to deal with on horseback. The Royalist authorities attempted to 'make do' by issuing 'powder bags' rather than bandoliers for musketeers to carry their gunpowder. The procedure for using the powder bag may have been that prescribed in a pre-war manual, where soldiers were warned not to load their muskets by taking a handful of powder and letting it trickle down the barrel. This would result in an unmeasured charge, which might explode the barrel or fail to project the bullet to its target.

J: Soldiers in siege lines

England in the 1640s lacked fortified towns and fortresses, but medieval town walls and castles were none the less reinforced and held, sometimes successfully, against besiegers who lacked both the necessary equipment and experience.

This chart from Ward's *Animadversions of Warre* provides the most widely quoted information about artillery of the period.

J1: Engineer

The term military engineer encompassed several levels of social standing and competence. At the highest level the engineer was an architect of military buildings and enjoyed great prestige, like Sir Bernard De Gomme, a notable figure in the retinues of King Charles and Prince Rupert. Lesser figures might find themselves involved in the practical construction of siegeworks, directing the manual labours of pioneers, soldiers and pressed civilians. Heavy suits of bullet-proof armour and helmets such as this were devised to enable engineers to work under fire.

The Names of the Peeces of great Ordnance now in most use.	The height of the Diameter of each Peece.	The height of the Bullet.	The weight of the shot in pounds.	Compasse of the shot in Inches and parts.	Weight of Serpentine Powder.	Weight of Corne Powder.	Weight of the Peece in Pounds.	Length of the Peece in Feet.	Thicknesse of Mettall at the Touch-hole, inches.	Thicknesse of the Mettall at the Trunnions.	Thicknesse of the Mettall at the Neck.	Ladles length.	Ladles breadth.	Length of the Plankes of the Carriage of the Peece.	Depth of each Planke in inches at fore-end.	Depth of the Planke at the lower end in feet.	Thicknesse of the Planke in inches and parts.	The number of men to draw each Peece in service.	The number of Horse to draw each Peece.	The number of yoke Oxen.	Distance of pace the Peece carries at point-blanke.	Distance of paces each Peece carries at utmost randon.	Length of the Coyler Ropes.
Canon of	8	7 1/6	64	25 1/7	40	32	8000	12	8	6 3/4	4	23 1/2	15	16 3/4	32	20	8	90	16	9	300	1500	70
Canon Serpentine.	7 1/2	6 3/4	52	23 4/7	25 1/4	26	7000	11 1/2	7 1/2	5 1/3	3 3/4	22	14 1/2	16 1/2	20	18 1/4	7 1/2	80	14	8	340	1600	66
French Canon.	7 1/4	7	46 3/4	22 11/14	25	23 3/4	6500	12	7 1/4	5 3/5	3 5/8	21	13 2/5	16 3/4	29	18	7 1/4	70	12	7	360	1740	64
Demi-Canon eldest.	6 3/4	6 1/2	36 5/8	21 1/14	20 1/4	20	6000	11 1/4	6 3/4	5 1/4	3 3/8	22	12	15 1/2	27	16 3/4	6 3/4	65	11	6	370	1800	60
Demi-Canon Ord.	6 1/2	6 1/4	32	20 2/7	20	18	5600	10 1/2	6 1/2	5	3 1/8	20	11 1/2	15 1/4	26	16 1/4	6 1/2	60	10	5	350	1700	54
Demi-Canon.	6	5 3/4	24 1/2	18 6/7	18	16	5000	11	6	4 1/2	3 1/10	21	11	16	24	15	6	56	9	5	340	1600	46
Culverin.	5 1/2	5 1/4	19	17 2/7	16	15	4500	13 1/4	7 1/2	4 1/2	3	22	9 1/2	18 1/4	22	13 5/8	5 1/2	50	8	4	420	2100	40
Ordinary Culverin.	5 1/4	5	16 1/4	16 1/2	15	12 1/2	4300	12	5 1/4	4 1/4	2 3/4	21	9	17 1/4	21	13 3/4	5 1/4	46	8	4	400	2000	36
Demi-Culverin.	4 1/2	4 1/4	11 1/4	14 1/7	9	9	3000	11	4 1/2	4	2 5/8	20	8 1/2	16 1/4	18	11 1/4	4 1/2	36	7	4	380	1800	34
Demi-Culverin lesse.	4 1/4	4	9	13 1/14	8	7 1/2	2300	10	4 1/4	3 1/4	2 2/3	19 1/2	7 1/4	14 5/8	17	10 3/4	4 1/4	28	6	3	320	1600	30
Saker ordinary.	3 3/4	3 1/2	5 1/4	11 11/14	5 1/2	5	1900	9 1/2	3 3/4	3 1/4	2 1/2	16	6 1/4	14	15	9 3/8	3 1/2	24	5	3	300	1500	28
Sakeret or Minion.	3 1/4	3	3 1/4	10 2/14	5	3 1/2	1100	8	3 1/4	2 1/4	2 1/4	14	5	11 1/2	13	8 1/4	2 1/2	20	4	2	280	1400	24
Fawcon.	2 3/4	2 1/2	2 1/3	8 2/14	2 1/2	2 1/4	750	7	2 1/4	2 1/3	2	12	4 1/2	10 1/4	11	7	2 1/4	16	3	2	260	120 0	20
Fawconet.	2 1/4	2	1 1/7	7 1/14	1 1/2	1 1/2	400	6	2 1/4	2	1 3/4	10	3 1/4	8 3/4	9	6 1/2	2 1/4	10	2	2	220	100	20
Rabinet.	1 1/2	1 1/4	3/4	3 3/4	3/4	2/4	300	5 3/4	1 1/2	1	1/2	9 1/2	2 1/2	7 1/2	8	5 1/2	2	8	2	2	150	700	18
Base.	1 1/4	1	1/2	3	1/3	1/4	200	4 1/4	1	1/2	1/4	8	2	6 1/2	7	5	2	6	2	2	100	560	18

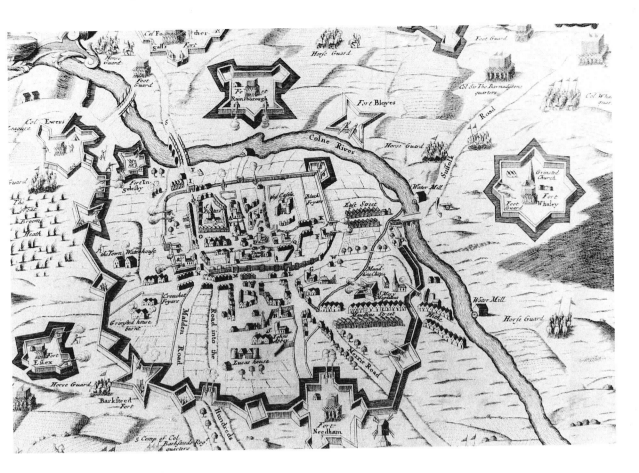

This view of the siege of Colchester shows both the medieval defences of the town and the forts and entrenchments of the besiegers. Note that only the forts are garrisoned, the main lines being patrolled by horse guards. (D. Carter collection)

J2: Cavalry trooper

Cavalrymen often took part in the final assault of the siege, firstly to justify their share in the plunder, but also because of their higher morale and better amour. In addition to his normal weapons this trooper has been given a pouch full of hand grenades with which to lead the assault. Ignited by a piece of burning matchcord and with a simple fuse, these could be as dangerous to the user as to the enemy.

J3: Gamekeeper turned sniper

The firearms issued to the common soldiers during the Civil Wars were cheap and inaccurate; but better weapons—many of them with rifled barrels—were available, often in the hands of civilian hunters or gamekeepers. The siege was a situation where the slow rate of fire of these weapons did not greatly matter, and both besieged and besiegers suffered from the attention of the accurate fire of these marksmen. Officers were a natural target and would often have to disguise their rank when appearing in the outworks. This man has retained the hunter's buff coat and leather gaiters (based upon a surviving example in the Cromwell Museum in Huntingdon) that he wore in civilian life.

K: The Artillery

The artillerist of the 17th century was a scientific adviser, and in many areas his expertise overlapped that of the engineer. Mathematical skill was needed to calculate ranges and trajectories, and the artillery expert protected his status with as much mystery and as many trigonometrical tables as possible. This artilleryman has obviously prospered from his expertise, for he has a richly decorated suit and embroidered baldric. He wears a heavily laced 'falling band' around his neck to protect his expensive clothes from becoming dirtied by his hair. On his head he wears a small cloth skull cap. Beside him stands a lindstock, holding the burning match and keeping it well out of the way while loose gunpowder is being used in the loading process.

Items (1) to (7) were used in the loading of a cannon. The lever (1) was used in the back-breaking task of moving the gun carriage, either to traverse the barrel or to run the cannon back to its firing position after it had recoiled. The rammer (2) was used to ensure that the powder and its retaining wad were securely packed into the barrel. Any gap between powder and ball could result in a build-up of explosive gasses which could rip open a cannon barrel with disastrous results for the crew. The wedge (3) was forced under the breech of the barrel to provide elevation. The ladle (4) was used to deliver a measured amount of gunpowder into the breech.

When the cannon had been fired it was necessary to use a swab (5) to wash out the barrel to prevent any dormant embers igniting the next charge prematurely, and to help cool the barrel. The pricker (6) was used to clear the touch hole of any powder residue, and the worm (7) for the dangerous task of removing a failed charge from the barrel. The next items of equipment were designed to tackle the problem caused by the fact that cannon barrels were not made to a standard size and each cannon ball had to be checked to make sure that it would fit. The holes in the gauge (8) corresponded to the diameter of the various cannons in a battery: if the shot passed through the appropriate hole it could be used in a given cannon. The dagger (9) was marked with graduations so that the correct shot could be selected. The compasses

The transportation of heavy siege guns was one of the greatest problems to beset the commanders of the Civil Wars. Movement on carriages such as this was very slow on the poor roads of the time, and movement by river was preferred whenever possible. (Dr. S. Bull collection)

The petard was a gunpowder-filled metal bell intended to be fitted to the gates of a fortress. Its shape and solidity directed the force of the explosion towards, and hopefully through, the door. (Dr. S. Bull collection)

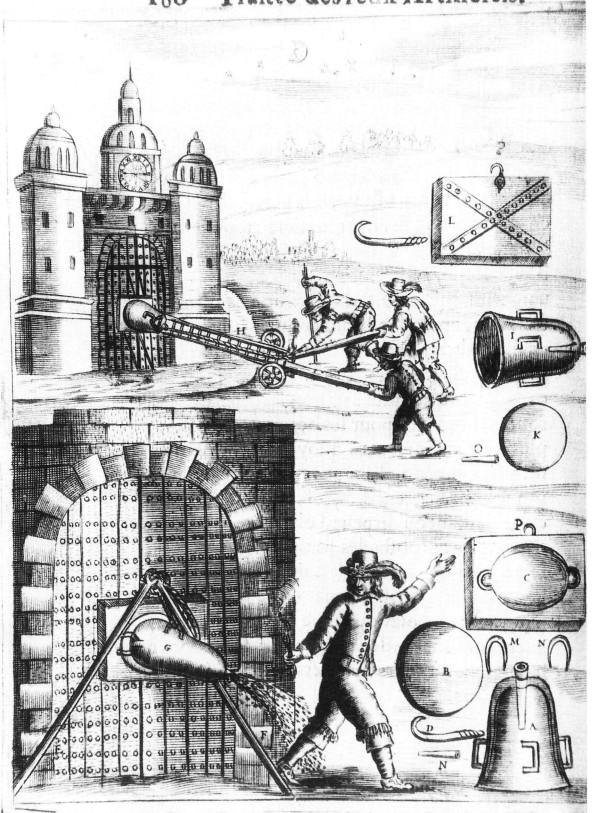

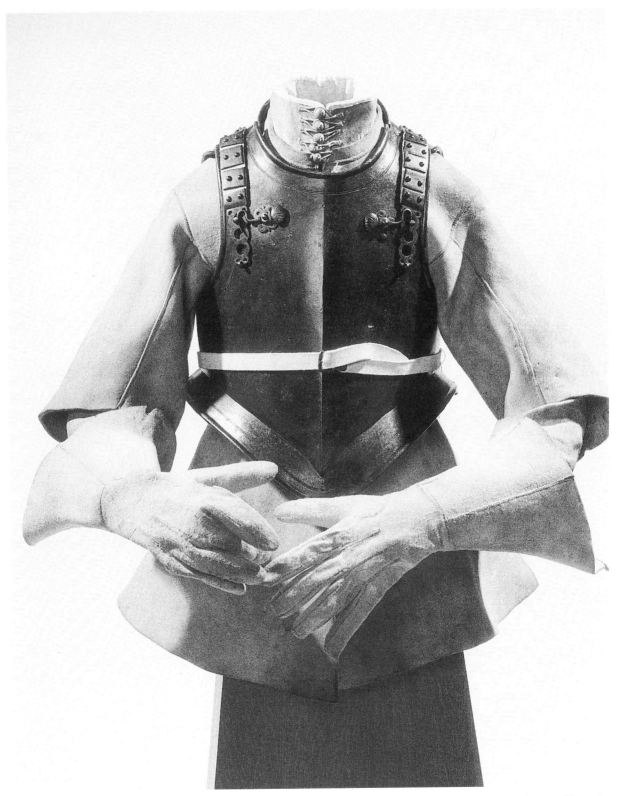

The firing of a mortar was an extremely dangerous task as both the fuse of the bomb itself and that of the mortar had to be lit. If the bomb fuse ignited but the propellant charge did not the bomb would explode, destroying the mortar and its crew! (Dr. S. Bull collection)

The buff coat and breast plate belonging to Alexander Popham from the Littlecote collection. The breastplate is of a much stronger construction than that issued to the ordinary soldier. (By courtesy of the Board of Trustees, Royal Armouries)

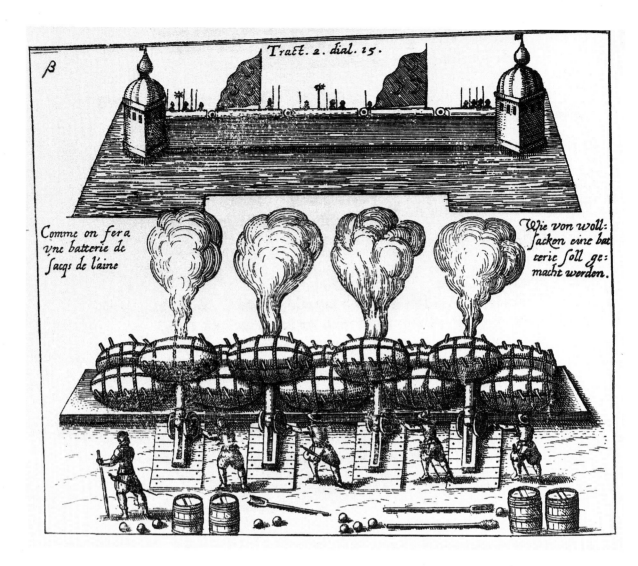

Traćt. 2. dial. 15.

β

Comme on fera
vne batterie de
sacqs de l'aine

Wie von woll:
sacken eine bat
terie soll ge:
macht werden.

(10) and calipers (11) were used to find the internal and external size of the barrel and shot. Many scales of measurement were used, and little attempt was made to check that the 'pound' used in one locality equalled the 'pound' used in the next. The wise gunner chose his shot with care. The last item (12) is a scale placed into the barrel of a cannon to determine its angle of elevation. When it was used in co-ordination with devices to

This siege battery from Ufano's *Artilleria* shows guns mounted on wooden platforms protected by bales of wool. Such guns were so heavy that without plank supports the recoil from each shot would dig them into the earth.

find the range to a target, the theorists promised a certain hit; but the poor quality of gun casting and powder production and the effects of wind and weather made gunnery much more of an art than a science.

Note some Granadoes are made of Canvaffe with divers Piftoll-barrels charged with powder and bullets, and covered over.

'Granados' for firing from mortars were usually made of brass, but some, designed to set buildings on fire, were made from canvas bags. The item marked B is the fuse which was inserted into the neck of the bag.

Notes sur les planches en couleur

A Ces campagnes étaient témoins aux dernières instances de l'usage dans les armées anglaises des chevaliers presque complètement armés. **A1**, **A2** Variants de l'helme 'clos'. **A3** Gorget, attaché par les tapes aux epaulières. Le plastron et la contreplaque (**A4**, **A6**) étaient capable d'être portes independament du reste de l'armure; les renforcements, placcarte et garde de reine, (**A5**, **A7**) étaient souvent écartés. Les cuisses, difficile à fabriquer, (**A8**), étaient les premiers articles à être écarté; des exemples en cuir au lieu d'acier sont connus. Les protections aux épaules et aux bras étaient souvent écartées en faveur d'un buff coat, quoiqu'un gant à manchette de gauche était souvent retenu pour proteger la main qui tenait les rènes. La maillotin, **A10**, était destiné à surmonter l'armure du cuirassier.

B La planche principale qui trouve dans le contenu survivant du magasin d'armes de Littlecote House, montre un cavalier de Popham's Troop. Autour de lui, variations de casque sont montrées. **B1** était un type commun dans les autre pays de L'Europe; **B7** était plus normale en Angleterre, quoique les barres n'étaient pas normales. **B2**, **B5**, **B6** sont des types européen; un petit nombre en était peut-être utilisé, quoiqu'ils sont tous chers, et **B2** est probablement un type officier. **B3** est probablement une adaptation d'un style surmodé; **B4** est grossièrement fabriqué par un forgeron de campagne, mais utilisable; **B8**, sont des secretes, portés au côté intérieur d'un chapeau en toile comme protection.

C1 Un costume et un 'chapeau-casque' dans le style français et un pistolet long. **C2** Le vieux gentilhomme a un costume – remarquez la collerette – et un accoutrement qui nous rappelent son service dans les guerres hollandaises quelques dizaines d'années avant. Beaucoup d'appareil surmodé était requisitionné par les armées indigentes. **C3** Le laquais, qui travail pour adapter une très vieille casque 'sallet', suivra ses maitres dans la guerre; sa manque d'equippage lui mettra dans le dernier rang de l'escadron.

D1 Un jeune officier de Sir Edward Peto's Troop, de Lord Brooke's Regiment, dans un costume civil personellement fourni, ce qui était normale pour les officiers. **D2** Le costume travaillé d'un sonneur de trompette était fourni par son colonel; remarquez le bonnet populaire 'Montero'. **D3** Remarquez le vieux casque burgonet, peindu noir pour ne pas se rouiller, un buff coat sans manches porté par-dessus le costume civil, et l'écharpe qui montrait sa soumission.

E1 Le 'manteau hollandais' était populaire par mauvais temps, et était souvent porté par-dessus l'armure pendant la bataille; remarquez encore le bonnet 'Montero'. **E2** Le cassack possédait des coutures par les côtés et par les manches en ou en manteau. **E3** Des manteaux simples de longeur variés étaient

Farbtafeln

A Diese Feldzüge waren die letzten Zeugen von fast völlig gepanzerten Rittern in Englischen Armeen. **A1**, **A2** Varianten des 'geschlossenen Helms'. **A3** Halsberge, mit Bändern an (**A9**) Schulterplatten befestigt. Es war möglich, den Brustharnisch und das Hinterstück, **A4**, **A6**, zusammengebunden und ohne die andere Panzerstücke zu tragen; die Verstärkungen, placcarte und garde de reine (**A5**, **A7**) wurden oft abgelegen. Die cuisses, die schwer zu machen waren, wurden oft die erste Stucke abgelegen zu werden; Exemplaren aus Leder statt Stahl sind bekannt. Die Schulter – und Armschütze wurden auch oft abgelegen und durch das buff coat ersetzt, obwohl ein Panzerhandschuh auf der linken Hand oft behalten wurde, um die Hand, die die Zügel hielt zu schützen. Der Kriegshammer, **A10**, war bestimmt, den Panzer des Kürassiers zu schlagen.

B Die Haupttafel, von dem übrigbleibenden Inhalt der Waffenkammer von Littlecote House genommen, zeigt einen Kavallerist von Popham's Troop. Ihm herum sehen wir verschiedene Arten Helme. **B1** war gewöhnlich in anderen europäischen Ländern; **B7** war gewöhnlich in England, obwohl die Verstärkunsstangen nicht gewöhnlich waren. **B2**, **B5**, **B6** sind europäisch; es waren vielleicht einige wenige davon in Gebrauch, obwohl alle teuer sind, und B2 ist wahrscheinlich ein Offiziershelm. **B3** ist wahrscheinlich eine Anpassung einer alten Mode; **B4** ist von einem dörflichen Schmied grob bearbeitet, aber brauchbar; **B8**, **B9** sind secretes, die als Schutz im Innern Stoffhüte getragen wurden.

C1 Kleidung und 'Hut-Helm' im französischen Stil und lange Pistole. **C2** Der alte Herr hat eine Kleidung – siehe die Halskrause – und eine Ausrüstung, die seinen Dienst viele Dekaden vorher in den holländischen Kriegen zurückrufen. Viele alte Ausrüstung wurde von den bedürftigen Armeen requiriert. **C3** Der Pferdeknecht, der arbeitet, einen alten 'sallet' Helm anzupassen, wird seinen Herren in den Krieg folgen; sein Ausrüstungsmangel wird ihn in dem ruckwärtigen Stab der Schwadron aufstellen.

D1 Junge Offizier von Sir Edward Peto's Troop von Lord Brookes' Regiment; er trägt eine selbstversorgte bürgerliche Kleidung, was bei Offizieren gewöhnlich war. **D2** Die sorgfältige Kleidung des Trompeters wurde von seinem Oberst besorgt; siehe die weitverbreitete Kappe 'Montero'. **D3** Siehe die alte Sturmhaube, schwarz gemalt gegen Rost, das ärmellose buff coat, über seine Kleidung getragen, und die Schärpe, die seine Treue zeigt.

E1 Der holländische Mantel war bei schlechtem Wetter beliebt, und wurde oft während der Schlacht über die Rüstung getragen; siehe noch einmal die Kappe 'Montero'. **E2** Das cassack hatte Säume mit Knöpfen an den Seiten und an den Ärmeln, und könnte als Mantel mit Ärmeln oder als loser Mantel

fournis pour la cavallerie en lieu des habits qui étaient portés par l'infanterie.

F Un impression de la défaite des 'homards' de Haselrigge's Regiment à Roundway Down; le drapeau est celui de la troupe du colonel même. Leurs ennemis royalistes, plus légèrement équipés comme 'harquebusiers' et en forme plus ouverte, montraient que les chevaliers étaient en effet finis. Quand même, l'armure protégeait les cuirassiers contre les coups de pistolets directs, et un officier royaliste qui avait tiré à plusieurs reprises et sans resultat sur un cuirassier, racontait que si le type avait été fourni avec des provisions, il aurait pu durer jusqu'au bout d'un siege.

G1 Un bon exemple d'un buff coat avec des rangs serrés de dentelle métallique sur les manches, l'origine de beaucoup de peintures incorrectes de troupes avec manches cerclées de couleurs sur les habits. La qualité et la coupe du habit font connaître qu'il est un officier. **G2** Remarquez l'effet chevauchant au front de la jupe de l'habit; ce buff coat ne s'ouvrait pas quand l'homme montrait à cheval, mais se tenait fermé pour couvrir la selle et les cuisses. Des indications de richesse et de rang sont le gorget et la belle casque de l'europe de l'est à l'épreuve des coups de mousquet 'Zischagge'. **G3** L'équipement classique d'un cavalier de la New Model Army – quoique c'était bien possible qu'en 1645 ils portaient leurs propres vêtements plûtot que des uniformes.

H1 Il existe une référence contemporaine à un officier dragon dans un habit rouge court, mais il n'y a pas de preuve que ce soit particulier aux dragons; les officiers de toutes armes portaient les vêtements de leur propre choix. **H2** Le dragon ne faisait pas des charges dans une bataille, ainsi sa selle ne possédait pas des soutiens en avant et en arrière. Remarquez la cartouchière. **H3** Les livres de comptes détaillent le longeur des mousquets des dragons, et ils précisent qu'ils étaient accrochés à un baudrier par des crochets à ressort. Il y a peu d'exemple pour l'illustration de leurs costumes; des chapeaux à larges bords sont montrés dans quelques engravures, mais le bonnet tricoté était également courant.

I1 Remarquez la large ceinture en cuir qui donnait de la protection supplémentaire au ventre; des écharpes rouges étaient normales pour les royalistes, mais beaucoup d'eux portaient des autres couleurs spécifiés par leurs officiers commandants. **I2** Costume typique d'un officier riche. **I3** Dragon mal-équipé, qui porte toujours un mousquet léger d'infanterie et du poudre dans un sac – incommode et dangereux tous les deux à manipuler à cheval.

J1 L'armure et les casques grosse épaisseur protégaient les ingénieurs contre feu d'ennemi. **J2** Les cavaliers étaient souvent enrôlés pour les assauts d'infanterie pendant les opérations d'un siège, à cause de leur armure supérieure; cet homme a un sac de grenades à utiliser dans un assaut, aussi dangereux pour lui que pour l'ennemi. **J3** Un garde-chasse, qui se bat maintenant comme canardeur et qui porte toujours son habit en cuir et ses guêtres de campagnard, avec un fusil de chasse juste.

K L'officier d'artillerie était un expert grassement payé, et les vêtements de cet homme sont un reflet de son rang social. Autour de lui sont les outils de l'artilleur. La plupart s'expliquent d'eux même. **K4** est un calibre pour les boulets de canon; les canons n'étaient pas fabriqués d'un calibre fixe, et au point de vue logistique c'était très difficile d'assurer qu'il y avait de la balle pour chaque calibre dans une batterie mixte. **K9**, **K10**, **K11** sont des appareils pour mesurer soit le calibre, soit la balle. **K12** est l'échelle, qu'on mettait dans la bouche du canon pour vérifier l'angle de mire.

geknöpft werden. **E3** Einfache Mäntel verschiedener Längen wurden für Kavallerie besorgt, statt der Mantel, die die Infanterie trug.

F Eine Darstellung der Niederlage der schwer gepanzerten 'Rotrocke' von Haselrigge's Regiment auf Roundway Down; die Fahne ist von der Abteilung des Obersts selbst. Ihre royalistische Feinde, als 'harquebusiers' leichter ausgerüstet und in offener Formation, bewiesen, daß es mit den Rittern vorbei war. Dennoch war die Rüstung ein Schutz wider Pistolenkernschuß; ein royalistischer Offizier erzählte, nachdem er immer wieder und erfolglos auf einen Kürassier geschossen hatte, daß wenn der Kerl mit Vorräten versorgt wäre, dann hätte er einer Belagerung standhalten können!

G1 Ein guter Beispiel des buffcoat, mit engen Reihen Metallitze auf den Ärmeln, wovon die viele irrigen Gemälde kommen, die Kavalleristen mit farbigen Bändern auf den Ärmeln zeigen. Die Qualität und der Schnitt des Rocks zeigen einen Offizier. **G2** Siehe die Überlappung auf der Vorderseite des Rocks; dieses buff coat öffnet nicht, wen der Mann aufs Pferd stieg, sondern zusammen blieb, um den Sattel und die Schenkel zu decken. Klasse- und Reichtumsanzeigen sind die Halsberge und der feine musketensichere osteuropäische 'Zischagge' Helm. **G3** Die klassische Ausrüstung eines Kavallerists des New Model Army, obwohl es möglich ist, daß sie in 1645 ihre eigenen Kleidungen statt Uniformen trugen.

H1 Es gibt einen gleichzeitigen Verweis auf einen Dragoneroffizier mit einem kurzen roten Rock, aber es gibt keinen Beweis, daß diese eigentümlich an Dragoner waren; Offiziere aller Gattungen trugen Kleider ihrer eigenen Wahl. **H2** Der Dragoner griff nicht im Sturmschnitt an, und sein Sattel hatte keine Bekräftigungen vorn und hinten. Siehe den Patronengurt. **H3** Rechnungsbücher geben die Länge Dragonermusketen, und bestimmen, daß sie mit Karabinerhaken an Wehrgehenken aufgehängt wurden. Es gibt wenige Beweise für ihr Kostüm; breitrandige Hüte sind auf einige Druckplatten gezeigt, aber es scheint, daß die gestrickte Kappe gleich gewöhnlich war.

I1 Siehe den breiten Ledergürtel, der weitere Schutz für den Bauch gab; rote Schärpen waren für Royalisten normal, obwohl viele davon andere von ihren Obersten bestimmte Farben trugen. **I2** Ein typisches Kostüm für einen reichen Offizier. **I3** Schlecht ausgerüsteter Dragoner, der eine Luntenschloßmuskete der Infanterie hat, und Pulver in einem Beutel trägt – sowohl peinlich als auch gefährlich zu Pferd zu gebrauchen.

J1 Schwere Rüstung und Helme schützten Pionieren unter feindlichem Beschuß. **J2** Kavalleristen wurden oft wegen ihrer besseren Rüstung für Infanteriesturmen während einer Belagerung eingezogen; dieser Mann hat einen Beutel voll Granaten, in dem Sturm zu benutzen; ihm ebenso wie dem Feind gefährlich. **J3** Ein Wildhüter, der jetzt als Scharfschütze kämpft, immer noch mit seinem bürgerlichen Lederrock und seinen Gamaschen, und mit einem genauen Jäger.

K Der Artillerieoffizier war ein teuer bezahlter Fachmann, und die Kleider dieses Mannes spiegelt seine Stellung. Ihm herum liegt das Werkzeug des Kanoniers. Es ist meistenteils selbstverständig. **K4** ist ein Gießlöffel – lockeres Pulver wird in die Mündung des Kanons eingelöffelt. **K8** ist ein Meßgerät für Kanonenkugeln; Kanonen wurden nicht zu gleichbleibenden Durchmessern gemacht, und es war vom logistischen Standpunkt aus sehr schwer, sicher zu sein, daß Kugeln verschiedener Größe in einer gemischten Batterie immer zur Verfügung waren. **K9**, **K10**, **K11** sind alte Geräte, die die Bohrung oder die Kugel maß. **K12** ist ein Maßstab, der in die Mündung gesetzt wurde, um den Steigungswinkel nachzusehen.